AF765160

Notting Hill Gate 3A

Workbook

Für Klasse 7 an Gesamtschulen und anderen integrierenden Schulformen

Diesterweg

Notting Hill Gate 3A

Workbook für Klasse 7 an Gesamtschulen und anderen integrierenden Schulformen

Differenzierende Ausgabe
Advanced Course

Herausgegeben von:
Dr. phil. h. c. Christoph Edelhoff, StD a. D.,
Vorsitzender THE ENGLISH ACADEMY

Erarbeitet von Michael Biermann, Otfried Börner, Hannelore Debus, Pamela Hanus, Phil Mothershaw-Rogalla, Ingrid Preedy, Kathleen Unterspann und Jürgen Wrobel, sowie Ruth Barker, Simone Collenberg, Ingrid Gebhard, Petra Günther, Pat Jüngst und Tanja Ripke
Fachliche Beratung: Natalie Beer, Lieselotte Bohnsack, Melanie Dahm, Arno Esser, Rolf-Olaf Geisler, Elvira van Haasteren, Susanne Hooß-Biehl, Stephanie Mayer, Angelika Pohlmann, Cornelia Scherer, Dr. Annegret Staufer, Noah Tauche und Michael Tetzlaff

Weitere Zusatzmaterialien zum Schülerbuch
(978-3-425-10603-8)

- Multimedia-Sprachtrainer 978-3-425-10653-3
- Audio-CDs für Schüler 978-3-425-10663-2
- Workbook mit Audio-CDs 978-3-425-10623-6
- Workbook mit Multimedia-Sprachtrainer 978-3-425-10633-5
- Workbook, Multimedia-Sprachtrainer und Audio-CDs 978-3-425-10643-4

Bildquellen:
S. 12 Indian Cuisine (Collections/Lawrence Engelsberg, London); S. 20 Andy Murray (Alamy/Franck Camhi); S. 24 Fußabdruck im Sand (Pixel-Kings (H.G.)/pixelio.de); S. 27 Fastnachtskostüme (12) (Jutta Eckardt-Scheurig, Wiesbaden); S. 28 Notting Hill Carnival (Alamy/John Sturrock), Frau in Hexenkostüm (Mauritius/Pokorski); S. 33 *Afroamerican slaves picking cotton* (AKG Images/akg/North Wind Picture Archives); S. 43 Impressionen Insel Spiekeroog (Nordseebad Spiekeroog GmbH); S. 51 Radio (mauritius images/Photo Alto), DVD (Cinetext Bildarchiv/Buena Vista, Frankfurt), Zeitung (PS Press/action press, Hamburg), Flugzeug (M. Jung, Frankfurt); S. 52 Technikmuseum Berlin; S. 56 Schneekugel (iStockphoto), Babuschka (fotolia), Origami (fotolia), Glückskatze (iStockphoto); S. 57 Glühbirne (Bildagentur Online), Reißverschluss (mauritius/Hackenberg), Kugelschreiber (P. King, München), Briefmarke (iStockphotos), Streichhölzer (Okapia, Frankfurt); S. 67 Bill Clinton (Ullstein), Celine Dion (Ullstein), J.K. Rowling (picture-alliance/dpa/epa), Eminem (picture-alliance/dpa/Anthony Harvey); S. 69 Cutty Sark (Alamy/Alex Segre), Canary Wharf Tower (iStockphoto/Roland Nagy); S. 73 Cartoon Flea Market (CartoonStock.com); S. 74 Pink im Konzert mit Fans (Corbis/Peter Kollanyi); S. 79 London International Gallery of Children's Art (LIGCA); S. 82 Paul Klee, *Senecio*; Andy Warhol, *Flowers*; Franz Marc, *Rehe im Wald II*; und Gabriele Münter, *Der blaue See* (4 x AKG images, Berlin); S. 83 Louise Bourgeois, *Maman* (Alamy/David Pearson), L.S. Lowry, *Coming out of school* (Tate Gallery, London), Marc Chagall, *The Blue Circus* (Alamy/Interfoto Fine Arts), Sean Henry, *Catafalque* (Alamy/Mike Booth), Pablo Picasso, Goat (Succession Picasso/VG Bild-Kunst, Bonn), René Magritte, *Empire of Light* (Cordon Art B.V. – Baarn-Holland); S. 93 Abflugtafel Flughafen (Wikimedia); S. 92 Ben Nevis (Alamy/Oxforshire).

Druck A^8 / Jahr 2015
Alle Drucke der Serie A sind im Unterricht parallel verwendbar.

Redaktion: Sabina Piatzer, Hannover, sowie Barbara Drauschke, Jutta Eckardt-Scheurig,
Dr. Katja Nandorf und Verena Nungesser
Herstellung: Harald Thumser, Frankfurt am Main
Illustrationen: Ulf Marckwort, Kassel
Umschlaggestaltung: Blum Design & Kommunikation, Hamburg
Satz: fotosatz griesheim GmbH, Griesheim
Druck und Bindung: westermann druck GmbH, Braunschweig

ISBN 978-3-425-**10613**-7

A1 ● Something to eat

a) Listen to A2 "In a restaurant" in your textbook again and number the pictures in the right order.

CD 1/1

b) Listen again and write the people's food under each picture.

c) Listen once more. Who says what? Write W for "waiter/waitress" and G for "guest" next to the speech bubbles.

CD 1/1

portfolio
I can listen

- Excuse me, could we have the bill, please?
- That's £25.50, please.
- Yes, I think so. How about you, Ann?
- Certainly, sir. Anything else?
- This restaurant was a good choice, wasn't it?
- What are you having?
- What's your food like? Is it good?
- What soft drinks have you got?
- Good evening. Are you ready to order?

d) Work with your partner and write a dialogue. Act it out.

Choose one of the pictures and describe the people and the restaurant.

portfolio
I can talk

A2 ● A menu

a) The menu for "The Green", a new restaurant in Notting Hill, is still empty. Fill in the dishes.

wordbank
food and drink

vegetable curry • mineral water • chicken soup • chocolate cake • lemonade • tomato salad • beef and onion pie • apple juice • sausage and chips • lemon pie • roast chicken • tea and coffee • fruit crumble • ham and melon • fish and chips • strawberry ice cream

Starters

__________ £ ____
__________ £ ____
__________ £ ____

Main courses

__________ £ ____
__________ £ ____
__________ £ ____
__________ £ ____
__________ £ ____

Desserts

__________ £ ____
__________ £ ____
__________ £ ____
__________ £ ____

Drinks

__________ £ ____
__________ £ ____
__________ £ ____
__________ £ ____

Tipp
Schau dir die Speisekarten in A1 im Textbook an.

b) Add the prices for the dishes.

c) Talk to a partner. Compare your prices.

A3 ● Can you remember?

a) Read A5 "Eating out?" in your textbook again. Then tick right, wrong or not in the text.

	right	wrong	not in the text
1. It's the first day of the holidays.	☐	☐	☐
2. Mrs Collins wants to eat a salad.	☐	☐	☐
3. Gillian eats a lot of cheeseburgers.	☐	☐	☐
4. Vanessa's favourite pizza is Ciao Bambino.	☐	☐	☐
5. Vanessa wants to pay for the meal.	☐	☐	☐
6. The Windsor has got tables outside.	☐	☐	☐
7. Mrs Collins and Gillian have been to Pizza World.	☐	☐	☐
8. Gillian has got a brilliant idea.	☐	☐	☐
9. Mrs Collins likes takeaway food.	☐	☐	☐

b) Correct the wrong sentences. Write the new sentences in your exercise book.

A4 ● Lots of things or not so many?

a) Complete the sentences with "much" or "many".

1. __________ people like to sit outside at the Windsor Castle.
2. How __________ money does Mrs Collins want to spend?
3. There isn't __________ cheese on Pizza Veneto.
4. How __________ pupils in your class can cook their own meals?
5. Gillian thinks she has eaten too __________ salad this week.
6. How __________ ice cream do you want to buy for the party?
7. Are there __________ takeaways in Notting Hill?
8. How __________ pizzas can you eat?
9. How __________ time have we got for this exercise?

LiF 1

portfolio I can work with grammar

b) Listen to the CD and check your sentences.

Make three sentences with "much" and three sentences with "many". Write them in your exercise book.

CD 1/2

A5 ● Partner interviews

a) Choose six things from the box and write down questions with "how much" and "how many" for your partner. You can also ask questions about other things.

How much milk do you drink?
How many English pop songs do you know?

milk • CDs • fast food • pop songs • tea • computer games • films • free time • comics • …

My questions	My partner's answers
How much	
How many	

LiF 1

b) Ask your partner and take notes on his or her answers. The answers can be:

- *a number: 3, 16, 25 …*
- *Not much. / Not many.*
- *Some.*
- *A lot.*

c) Report some facts to the class.

portfolio I can talk

A6 ● At the Windsor Castle

1/4

a) The Johnson family are having lunch at the Windsor Castle. Listen to the dialogue and answer the questions.

how to ... listen

What day is it? ____________________

What is the weather like? ____________________

Where are the Johnsons sitting? ____________________

____

Tipp
Schau dir während du zuhörst die Windsor Castle Speisekarte (TB S.12) an.

b) Listen again and tick the right statements.

1. Jack says that
- [ ] it is too hot to have curry.
- [ ] Indians eat curry every day.
- [ ] Indians eat chicken every day.

2. At first Rita wants
- [ ] vegetarian lasagna.
- [ ] ice cream.
- [ ] fish pie.

3. Mrs Johnson orders
- [ ] tomato soup and melon salad.
- [ ] vegetable soup and garden salad.
- [ ] soup of the day and melon salad.

4. Susan orders
- [ ] a main course with meat.
- [ ] vegetarian lasagna.
- [ ] garden salad, tomato soup and garlic bread.

Read the questions, listen again and take notes. Then answer the questions.

1. Why does Susan just want to eat some starters? ____________________

____

2. What does Jack say about the weather in India? ____________________

____

3. What does Rita want to eat first? ____________________

4. Mrs Johnson suggests vegetarian lasagna for Rita. Why? ____________________

____

5. What does Mrs Johnson order? ____________________

6. Who will have fish pie? ____________________

7. What do the Johnsons drink? ____________________

____

A7 ● In a German restaurant

You are in a German restaurant with an English friend. He doesn't speak German so you have to help him. Write down what you say.

how to … help out in English

Kellner: Hallo. Möchtet ihr schon bestellen?

Du: Are you ready to order? ______

Dein Freund: I'm not sure what to eat. Have they got sausage and chips?

Du: Haben Sie ______

Kellner: Wir haben heute nur Hähnchen mit Pommes frites.

Du: ______

Dein Freund: I don't like chicken. What about fish? Have they got fish and chips?

portfolio I can help out in English

Du: ______

Kellner: Tut mir leid. Wir haben keinen Fisch mehr. Aber es gibt auch Pizza und Spaghetti.

Dein Freund: I understood him, I think. Did he say they've got pizza and spaghetti?

Du: ______

Dein Freund: Then I'd like pizza with ham and olives.

Du: ______ Und ich möchte Spaghetti Bolognese.

Kellner: Wie sieht's mit Getränken aus?

Du: ______

Dein Freund: I'll have an apple juice.

Du: ______ und ein Wasser, bitte.

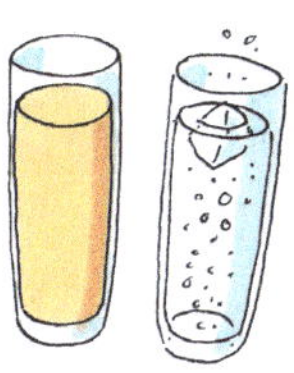

Kellner: Habt ihr noch einen Wunsch?

Du: ______

Dein Freund: No, that's fine, thanks.

Du: ______

A8 ● Sound check

a) Mark the stress in these words. The stress for "supermarket" has already been done for you.

supermarket	director	business	restaurants	Hong Kong
appetite	interesting	stomach	understand	enjoyable

Tipp Benutze einen Bleistift.

b) Listen to the story about Rosemary in your textbook again and check your stresses.

c) Now read the words aloud with correct stresses.

CD 1/5 1/4

A9 Have you ever …?

LiF
2, 3R

a) Work in groups of four. Who has or hasn't done these things in your group? Ask each other and note down your group members' answers in the grid.

how to …
talk

Have you ever | camped in the garden / met a film star / read a book in English / stayed in bed all day / seen a ghost | ?

Yes, I have, but only once.

Yes, I have. That was last summer. My friend and I camped in our garden for three days.

No, I've never done that.

	name	how often	more info
camped in the garden			
met a film star			

b) Report to the class about your list.

c) Write about the most interesting facts in your exercise book.

Murat has never read a book in English but he has read many English comics.
Nadine has been to Australia. That was in 2008. Her aunt lives there.
Dominik, Marco and Hatice have often …

A10 ● The strangest food

a) Rajiv wants to know more about the food Rosemary has eaten in other countries. Put the verbs into the present perfect or the simple past.

Rajiv: Tell me more about your trips to other countries.

__________ you ever __________ to Thailand? (be)

Rosemary: Yes, I ______________ there once. (be) It __________ wonderful. (be)

Rajiv: __________ you __________ the food there? (like)

Rosemary: Oh yes, very much. I __________ some really delicious vegetable dishes there. (have)

Rajiv: What __________ the best foreign food you __________ ever ___________? (be, eat)

Rosemary: Last year my dad and I __________ home-made ravioli with tomato sauce in a small restaurant in Rome. (have) The food __________ delicious. (taste)

Rajiv: And __________ you ever __________ something really strange? (eat)

Rosemary: Yes, but that _____________ in a foreign country. (not be) It _____________ here in London. (be) A friend _____________ me to her house some months ago. (invite) You will never guess what she _____________ (serve): cheeseburgers with strawberry jam on top. She also _______________ me a milkshake and _____________ me to dip my chips into it. (offer, tell) It __________ the most awful food I __________ ever __________. (be, have)

Rajiv: Ugh, that's horrible!

b) Listen to the CD and check your text.

LiF 2R, 3

LiF 4

portfolio: I can learn English

CD 1/5

A11 ○ Choose

1. **Write a text about some strange food you have eaten. Describe the food and say where you had it.**
2. **You want to surprise your friends with some very special food. What do you serve them? Plan a meal and describe it. If you like, give your dishes special names.**
3. **Write a text about a funny or a strange situation in a restaurant, for example when you did not get the food you ordered or the waiters did not serve you. Describe your reaction, too.**

My brother loves marshmallows. One day he wanted to surprise us with a "special" marshmallow dish. He mixed a bag of marshmallows with cream and big pieces of chocolate. Then he put everything into the oven. My parents and I ate my brother's "special dish" and told him that we liked it. But we felt awful because the food was really sticky and sweet.

wordbank: food and drink

Model

portfolio: I can write, I can learn English

B1 ● At Rajiv's house

CD 1/7 1/6

a) Listen to the CD and underline the words that are wrong.

Rajiv is a great cook and he loves eating. He wants to invite some classmates for a real Indian meal.

Rajiv: I'm making a curry on Sunday. And lots of banana pudding. Do you want to come round?

Vanessa: Oooh, sounds great. I can help with the cutting, can't I?

Rajiv: Yeah, why not. I'm inviting Susan and Rosemary, a girl I know from the supermarket, and perhaps Charlie. We could all work together.

portfolio
I can listen

Vanessa: That would be fantastic!

On Saturday Rajiv's house is crowded.

Gillian: Mmm. Smells nice, doesn't it?

Rajiv: I always make it the way my grandmother did. When she first came over from India, she brought lots of food with her.

Charlie: I thought you could buy everything at the superstore.

Rajiv: Well, now you can. But when she arrived here, people had no idea about Indian food. Now there are lots of Asian supermarkets and I can buy all the things I need.

CD 1/7 1/6

b) Listen again and write down the correct words.

c) Look at B1 "Rajiv's curry party" in your textbook and check your spelling.

B2 ● Who likes the curry?

a) Read B1 "Rajiv's curry party" in your textbook again and find out what the children think about the curry. Draw ☺, 😐 or ☹ and explain.

how to ... read

Rajiv	☺	*likes hot curry, thinks it is funny that*
Gillian		
Vanessa		
Rosemary		
Charlie		

b) Work with a partner. Make notes for a dialogue between Rajiv and Rosemary OR between Vanessa and Charlie. What do they say about Rajiv's curry party the next day?

c) Act out your dialogue.

B3 ● You can do it, can't you?

a) Find the right question tags. Add them to the sentences.

1. Mrs Patel is very friendly, ______________________?
2. Charlie loves his goldfish, ______________________?
3. You have got a green bike, ______________________?
4. Susan went to the disco last Saturday, ______________________?
5. We can go in-line skating tomorrow, ______________________?
6. You often help your parents in the house, ______________________?
7. Your dad did this maths exercise for you, ______________________?
8. Miriam collects animal posters, ______________________?
9. Apple crumble is a typical English dessert, ______________________?
10. Rosemary and her father often eat foreign food, ______________________?

LiF 4

portfolio
I can work with grammar

b) Listen to the CD and check your sentences.

CD 1/8

Work with a partner. Each of you has got a sheet of paper. One of you writes down a sentence. The other one writes down a question tag. Then swap your sheets and add the missing sentence part. Do this three or four times.

B4 ○ Food, glorious food

how to ...
work with a dictionary

a) Read these verses from a song. Look up new words in a dictionary.

b) Add new food words from the song to your word web from B4 in your textbook.
You can add these categories: • **hot meals** • **desserts** • **ways to cook food**

wordbank
food and drink

c) Now listen to the whole song. It is from the musical, *Oliver*. Why do the boys sing about "glorious food"? Take notes and describe the boys' situation.

CD 1/9 1/9

____

____

____

B5 ○ Choose

how to … write

1. Close your eyes and imagine delicious kinds of food. What are they? Make a list. Then compare your list with a partner's.
2. Have you ever been very hungry? What was it like? How long did you have to wait until you could eat something? How did you feel when you finally got some food? Write a text about the situation.
3. Write about a meal you enjoyed very much. Where and when did you have it? What did you eat? How did you feel when you ate it?

B6 ○ Indian food in Britain

a) Read the text and then complete the sentences.

how to … read

Many Indians live in Britain, so Indian food has become more and more popular there. You can find Indian takeaways or restaurants in most towns. British people's favourite take-away dish is no longer fish and chips, but Chicken Tikka Masala. They often just call this spicy dish CTM. Curries are also very popular. They are meals with vegetables or meat in a special sauce. You eat them with rice.
A lot of dishes you get in Indian restaurants in Britain are a bit different from original Indian food because they are sweeter and milder. Traditionally, Indians use a lot of different spices, some of which are really hot, for example chillies and different kinds of pepper. One very hot dish is curry vindaloo. Quite a few people find it delicious, but for others eating it can be a test of courage[1].

[1] test of courage – *Mutprobe*

1. You can find a lot of Indian restaurants in Britain because ______________________

____

2. Chicken Tikka Masala is ______________________

____

3. Curries are ______________________

____

b) Find words in the text that describe how food can taste. Write them down.

Tipp
Du kannst ein Wörterbuch benutzen.

sweet, ____

____

c) Think of different kinds of food and add more words to your list from b). Look at the lyrics in B4 again, too.

d) With a partner, talk about different kinds of food you like and don't like. Describe how they taste.

I think mushrooms taste terrible. I never eat them.

Oh, really? I think they taste wonderful. For example, I love pizza with mushrooms.

B7 ● How to make vegetable curry

a) Read the recipe and number the pictures in the right order.

1. Cut an onion and fry it in 1 tbsp. of oil.
2. Add 2 tbsp. of curry paste.
3. Add 400g canned tomatoes and 1 bag of frozen mixed vegetables.
4. Add 200ml water and cook the curry slowly for 15–20 minutes until the vegetables are well done.
5. Season with salt and pepper.
6. Serve with rice.

b) Explain in German how to make vegetable curry.

Write down your favourite recipe in English. If you like, add some pictures.

how to … help out in English

portfolio I can help out in English

B8 ○ Different ways of eating

Read B6 "Eating habits" in your textbook twice. Then close the book and match the countries to the information. Write down the right numbers below.

A In Britain
B In Iran
C In Italy
D In New Guinea
E In China
F In France
G In India
H In Japan
I In Switzerland

1 you must never cut spaghetti.
2 they often have cheese fondues.
3 people sometimes eat snails.
4 they cut vegetables into very small pieces for their sauces.
5 a lot of people like raw fish very much.
6 people like meat and potatoes.
7 they usually serve food on a large cloth on the floor.
8 some people cook their food in an oven in the ground.
9 there is a special way to eat peas.
10 people use chapati to pick up their food.
11 they use chopsticks to eat their meals.

Tipp
Es gibt mehr Informationen als du benötigst.

A		B		C		D		E		F		G		H		I	

D1 Look through Theme 1 in your textbook. Who is it?

She pays £25.50 for lunch: That's ______

She eats her food with her fingers: ______

She is wearing a white coat and is buying some Indian food: ______

She is carrying five plates: ______

D2 Choose a three-course meal from the Windsor Castle menu and one drink.
How much is the meal in pounds? How much would you have to pay for it in euros?

My three-course meal: ______

______

______

Drink: ______

Price in £: ______ Price in €: ______

D3 Go through Theme 1 in your textbook again and find the pictures.

1. You can see one white shoe on page ______.
2. The Queen is on page ______.
3. You can see different soft drinks on pages ______.
4. There is a bee on page ______.
5. You can see spaghetti and olives in a picture on page ______.

D4 Look at "People and places" on page 19 in your textbook again. What do these figures stand for?

1.12 billion: ______

300: ______

15: ______

80%: ______

1/5: ______

D5 What did the hungry computer eat?

Chips, one byte at a time.

A1 Miss Fitness and Miss Couch Potato

a) Look at the pictures and write about each woman. Use these phrases:

only like sports on TV • go jogging at the weekend • often lie on the sofa • eat lots of burgers and crisps • do gymnastics in the morning • always take the lift • walk a lot • eat healthy food • usually go into town by car • go to the gym three times a week

Miss Fitness ______________________

____

____

____

____

Miss Couch Potato ______________________

____

____

____

____

b) Are you a "fitness type" or a "couch potato type"? Talk to a partner and say why.

c) How can Miss Couch Potato become fitter? Write down five tips for her.

____

____

____

____

____

Compare your life with Miss Fitness's life. Could you do the same things to stay fit? What is possible for you? What don't you want to do? Write down your ideas.

I could go jogging at the weekend.
I can't do gymnastics in the morning because I have to go to school.
I don't want to go to a gym because it's too expensive.

____

____

____

____

____

d) Work with a partner. Imagine Miss Fitness and Miss Couch Potato meet at a party. Make notes for a dialogue. Then act it out in class.

portfolio
I can talk

A2 ● Gillian's exercises

portfolio
I can read,
I can work
with words

a) **Gillian goes to a hip hop class twice a week. They always have to do some exercises at the beginning of the class. Read the instructions[1]. Then write the right instructions next to the pictures.**

Exercise 1:
Stand straight with your feet together.
Stretch[2] your arms above your head.
Now bend[3] forward slowly and touch your toes.

Exercise 2:
Stand straight with your feet apart[4].
Touch your left foot with your right hand.
Stand straight again.
Touch your right foot with your left hand.

Exercise 3:
Stand straight with your feet apart.
Lift your right arm and bend to the left.
Stand straight again.
Lift your left arm and bend to the right.

CD 1/12

b) **Now listen to the CD and do the exercises.**

portfolio
I can write

c) **Think of a new exercise and make notes. Then tell a partner what to do.**

[1]instruction – *Anweisung;* [2]stretch – *strecken;* [3]bend – *beugen;* [4]apart – *auseinander*

A3 ● Jennifer's favourite sport

CD 1/13 1/15

a) ☆ **Listen to Jennifer from A3a) "Favourite sports" in your textbook again. Underline the words she uses.**

crazy   famous   favourite   late   great   read   red

scarf   last   fast   exciting   action   friends   fantastic

fans   change   chants   players   plays   win   game

Listen to Jennifer from A3a) "Favourite sports" in your textbook again. Then answer the questions.

CD 1/13 1/15

1. What colour are the Calgary Flames' shirts? ______________________________
2. What does Jennifer wear when she watches the Flames? ______________________________
3. Why does Jennifer like live games? ______________________________
4. What do the fans do when the Flames are playing? ______________________________

____

A4 Basketball and netball

a) Read Kellie's text in A3 "Favourite sports" in your textbook again. What do you find out about netball? Take notes.

____

____

____

b) Work with a partner and use the Internet. One person finds out the rules of netball, and the other one finds out the rules of basketball. What is the same? What is different? Together, make a list like this:

netball and basketball	
same rules	differences

how to … use the Internet

c) Present the information to another pair. Compare what you have found out.

A5 Which sports do you like watching?

a) Interview five classmates. Which sports do they like watching? Where do they watch them? Why do they like them?

I like watching basketball in a gym because the atmosphere is great.

I like watching football on TV because it's exciting.

portfolio I can talk

Make notes like this:

Sven – football – TV – exciting

Melanie – basketball – gym – great atmosphere

LiF 5

name	likes watching	where	why

portfolio I can talk

b) Report to the class.

Sven likes watching …

A6 ● Do you like it or hate it?

CD 1/16
portfolio I can listen
LiF 5

a) Listen to Gillian talking about sports. What does she like? What doesn't she like? Fill in the words.

Gillian likes ____________________ .

She doesn't like ____________________ some of the warm-up exercises.

For example, she hates ____________________ on the spot.

But she thinks ____________________ and ____________________ are OK.

b) When doing sports, what do *you* like? What don't *you* like? Fill in the gaps.

run • jump • stretch • hop • walk • bend • dance • step • swim • …

wordbank sports
portfolio I can work with grammar

I like ______________________________

I don't mind[1] ______________________________

I enjoy ______________________________

I love ______________________________

But I don't like ______________________________

And I don't enjoy ______________________________

I dislike ______________________________

And I hate ______________________________

[1] I don't mind … – *Ich habe nichts gegen …*

A7 ● Fast, faster, fastest

LiF 6R

a) Fill in the missing forms.

fast – faster – fastest	popular – more popular – most popular
tall – –	exciting – –
– younger –	– more powerful –
– – cleverest	– – most muscular
fit – –	professional – –
crazy – –	– more skilful –
– – highest	– – most brilliant
slim – –	special – –
– bigger –	– more beautiful –
– – best	– – most successful

b) ☆ Find more adjectives and make a grid like this for your partner.

☼ Compare sports stars who do the same sport, for example three football players, three swimmers and three runners.

I think … is more skilful than … But … is the most skilful football player.

A8 ● Sound check

a) Read these sports words and write them down.

[kə'rɑːti]	['præktɪs]	['pleɪə]	['mʌskjʊlə]	[eə'rəʊbɪks]
______	______	______	______	______
['krɪkɪt]	['gəʊlˌkiːpə]	[sək'sesfəl]	[breθ]	['konsnˌtreɪt]
______	______	______	______	______

b) Listen to the CD and check your words.

CD 1/17

A9 ○ Chants

CD 1/19 1/20 1/21

a) Listen to the three basketball chants on CD. Then choose one and practise speaking it in a group.

b) Speak your chant in front of the class.

With a partner, write a chant for your favourite sport. Present it in class.

We want it up
And in
And over the rim[1]!

Dribble it
Pass it
Let's make a basket!

Down down down the floor
Raise raise raise the score
Down the floor
Raise the score
Two points more!

[1] rim – *Rand (des Basketballkorbs)*

A10 ○ Hidden words

Look at the German words in the blue box. Then find the English words for them in the hidden word puzzle. → ←↓↑↘ ↙

E	B	T	S	E	T	J	S	K	Z	R	I	A	N	W	A
R	A	L	U	P	O	P	Q	E	T	D	V	D	P	O	L
E	M	I	T	E	E	R	F	N	A	J	T	A	U	N	H
R	G	N	I	Z	A	M	A	W	Y	S	V	E	O	D	T
V	R	E	P	E	X	N	O	T	E	R	O	L	X	E	A
A	C	A	G	M	E	A	N	I	N	G	K	N	M	R	E
Z	I	U	Y	E	T	A	R	T	N	E	C	N	O	C	R
N	I	N	J	U	R	Y	G	N	I	T	I	C	X	E	B

aufregend, spannend
Freizeit
Bedeutung
führen
Atem
erstaunlich, toll
Luft
sich konzentrieren
Schmerz
Verletzung
beliebt
Jahreszeit, Saison
sich fragen
prüfen
Notiz

A11 ○ Choose

1. Make a hidden word puzzle with sports words. Your partner has to find the words.
2. Make a list with sports you can do • alone • with a partner • in a team
   Present your list in class.
3. In a group, play a game. Take turns describing a sport. The others have to guess what it is.

It is a ball game. You play it in a team. You play it indoors.

A12 Becoming a winner

how to … read, work with a dictionary

a) Read about Andy Murray. Look up new words in a dictionary.

Andrew (Andy) Murray is a professional tennis player and member of the British Davis Cup team. He was born in Dunblane, Scotland, on May 15th, 1987. Andy is 1.90 m tall. He plays a double-handed backhand and won his first important title, the Orange Bowl, in Florida at the age of twelve. Five years later he won the junior US Open. He was second in the 2008 US Open. Andy lives in London.

Why did you become a professional tennis player?
When I was very young, I just enjoyed playing. I loved watching Andre Agassi and I had the same clothes: the jeans shorts with the pink shorts underneath, and even a cap with a blond pony tail on it! When I was 14, I wanted to become a professional tennis player. I decided to leave Scotland and live in Spain. That's when I started to train hard.

What do you need to become a champion in your sport?
You need to have a strong character and a strong body to get to the very top and stay there. You also have to be a good tactical thinker and be able to solve your problems on your own. Each point in a tennis match is a problem to solve!

How important is hard work?
You can't get to the top on talent alone. You need to work hard and practise on court and in the gym. Since I was 15, I've trained about five hours a day.

What does "winning" mean to you?
Winning is finding a way to overcome every challenge.

b) Fill in words from the text.

1. When you play a sport as a job, you are a ______________ player.
2. A ______________ is a building or club where you do exercises.
3. A ______________ is someone who has won an important competition.
4. If you are able to do something really well, you have got ______________ .

c) Complete the sentences.

portfolio – I can read

1. When Andy was young, he loved ______________
2. At the age of 14 ______________
____
3. Andy thinks that a champion needs ______________
____
4. Since Andy was 15, ______________

portfolio – I can write

d) Make a fact file about Andy Murray and present it in class. Use these categories:
- **home country** • **lives in** • **born on** • **born in** • **height**
- **career** • **other information**

Find information about another sportsperson. Then write a short report about his or her career.

B1 ● Seeing the doctor

a) What health problems can you have with different body parts? How would you talk about them? Use the words from the box.

I've got …

I can't …

I've broken/ cut my …

My … is aching/hurts.

hurt • aching • broken • headache • bruised • sore • backache • swollen • move • torn • stomach ache • cut

portfolio
I can work with words

b) Fill in the list.

head: *My head is aching. / I've got a headache. /* ______

back: ______

hand: ______

leg: ______

stomach: ______

foot: ______

wordbank
health

B2 ● How to help out at the doctor's

The girl doesn't speak German. How does the boy help out? Write down what he says.

how to …
help out in English

portfolio
I can help out in English

B3 ● Helping out at the doctor's

CD 1/23

portfolio I can listen

a) Katie, an English girl, is visiting you. She has a health problem. What is wrong with her? What happened? Listen to her and take notes.

____

____

____

____

____

b) Imagine you have to explain Katie's problem to a German doctor. What do you say?

B4 ● Role plays

Work with a partner and act out the scene.

Partner A: Patient/Patientin

1 Begrüße B und stelle dich vor.

3 Sage, dass du dich am linken Arm verletzt hast und ihn nicht bewegen kannst.

5 Antworte, dass du Basketball gespielt hast und dabei hingefallen bist.

7 Frage, ob du einen Verband oder Medizin brauchst.

Partner B: Arzt/Ärztin

2 Begrüße A und frage, was er/sie hat.

4 Frage, was passiert ist.

6 Sage, dass du den Arm sehen möchtest.

8 Antworte, dass du den Arm erst einmal röntgen musst. Dann werdet ihr sehen, was das Problem ist.

portfolio I can talk

Work with a partner and act out the scene.

Partner A: Patient/Patientin

1 Begrüße B und stelle dich vor.

3 Sage, dass du einen Fahrradunfall hattest und auf den rechten Arm gefallen bist.

5 Antworte, dass es sehr weh tut und dass du denkst, der Arm ist gebrochen.

7 Sage, dass du froh bist, dass der Arm nicht gebrochen ist. Frage, wann du wieder Sport treiben kannst.

9 Sage, dass das schrecklich ist, weil du in einem Basketballverein bist und am Samstag ein Spiel stattfindet. Dann frage, ob du noch mal kommen musst.

11 Bedanke und verabschiede dich.

Partner B: Arzt/Ärztin

2 Begrüße A und frage, was er/sie hat.

4 Sage, dass du den Arm ansehen möchtest. Taste den Arm ab und frage, ob das weh tut.

6 Sage, dass der Arm nicht gebrochen, sondern nur geprellt ist. Gib A eine Salbe und sage, dass sie helfen wird.

8 Sage, dass er/sie Fußball spielen oder joggen kann. Aber er/sie darf keinen Sport treiben, bei dem er/sie die Arme benutzen muss.

10 Antworte, dass er/sie in einer Woche wiederkommen soll.

12 Verabschiede dich.

B5 Choose

1. Write an e-mail for Charlie in which he tells Vanessa about his accident and his visit to the doctor's.
2. Charlie tells his parents about the accident and his visit to the doctor's. In groups of three, make notes for a dialogue. Then act it out.
3. What did Charlie do the next day? Write a short text.
4. When Charlie comes home, he can't use his right hand because his finger is bruised. So he asks his sisters, Josephine and Sharon, to do a lot of things for him. How do they react? Draw a comic.
5. Work with a partner. Choose another health problem and make notes for a dialogue. Practise it and act it out in class.

B6 In the waiting room

a) Look at the picture in B2 "What's the problem?" in your textbook and listen to the CD again. Then tick right or wrong.

CD 1/16

	right	wrong
1. The man in the blue pullover was in a forest when a dog came along.	☐	☐
2. He was jogging when the dog bit him.	☐	☐
3. The blond young woman was also jogging when she hurt her foot.	☐	☐
4. The young woman stepped on some broken glass in the park.	☐	☐
5. This happened to her yesterday morning.	☐	☐
6. The woman with backache had an accident at home.	☐	☐
7. She wanted to get a DVD off the top shelf.	☐	☐
8. The old lady had something wrong for lunch yesterday.	☐	☐

Look at the picture in B2 "What's the problem?" in your textbook and listen to the CD again. Then answer the questions.

1. Where was the man in the blue pullover when the dog bit him?

____

2. Why did the blond young woman hurt her foot?

____

3. Why did the woman with the white shirt hurt her back?

____

4. Why has the old lady got a stomach ache?

____

5. Two people don't tell the others about their problems. Who are they?

____

b) Correct the wrong sentences from a) in your exercise book.

Write down in your exercise book what the other two people could say about their problems.

B7 ● Life can be dangerous

a) Write down what has happened.

LiF 7

____

____

portfolio
I can work with grammar

b) Look at the pictures again. What aren't the people able to do? Write down your ideas.

1. *The boy isn't able to* ______________________
2. ______________________
3. ______________________
4. ______________________
5. ______________________
6. ______________________

B8 ○ Your left foot

a) What are you able to do with your left foot? Find out at home and tick your answers.

LiF 7

Are you able to …	yes	no
… pick things up from the floor with your left foot?		
… draw pictures with your left foot?		
… eat with your left foot?		
… type on the computer with your left foot?		
… switch on the TV with your left foot?		

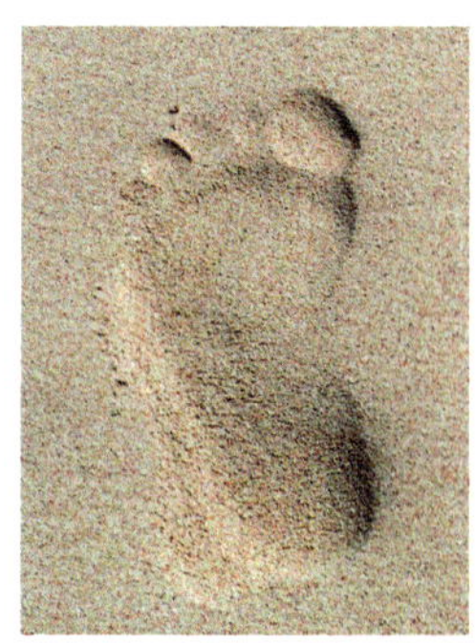

What else are you able to do with your left foot? Find out and make notes.

____

____

b) Tell the class what you have found out.

B9 Easy or difficult?

a) Read B4 "The story of Christy Brown" in your textbook again. Then fill in these words:

writing • reading • feeding • putting

________________ himself or ________________ on his clothes was not possible[1] for Christy. ________________ was no problem and ________________ was only possible with his left foot.

[1] possible – *möglich*

LiF 5

b) What was easy, difficult or not possible for Christy? Write your ideas in your exercise book. The phrases in the box will help you.

draw pictures • brush his teeth • travel • turn on the radio • make phone calls • listen to music • go swimming • …

I think … was easy for him.
Perhaps …

B10 What could you do?

a) Can you remember times when you were ill? What could you still do? What couldn't you do? Fill in the table.

When I had …	I could	I could not
a cold		
a headache		
a toothache		

LiF 7

b) Talk to a partner.

When I had a headache, I could watch TV, but I couldn't do my homework.

B11 When you were five

What were you able to do when you were five years old? What weren't you able to do? Write down what you remember.

speak English | ride a bicycle | climb a tree | use a computer | play football | …

When I was five years old, I was able to ________________ *, but I wasn't able to* ________________

I was able to ________________

____

____

____

LiF 7

D1 Do these exercises.

Jump up and down for one minute.
Do 15 press-ups.
Lift your arms and swing them forward eight times.
Touch the floor with your fingers. Do this ten times.

D2 Make a list of the English words in Theme 2 that look or sound similar in German.

sport, fitness, blind, ______________________________

____

____

D3 Look at the pictures in Theme 2. Where can you find these people and things?

stairs: page ______________

a football goal: page ______________

a runner without legs: page ______________

a box on wheels: page ______________

bikes: pages ______________

two people who are dancing: page ______________

the motto "A GOOD NAME ENDURETH": page ______________

D4 Odd one out – but why?

1. fitter – player – faster – cleverer ______________ is not a comparative[1].
2. walking – travelling – sing – dancing ______________ is not an ing-form.
3. helmet – gymnasium – stadium – pool ______________ is not a place where you do sports.
4. exciting – awesome – watching – excited ______________ is not an adjective.
5. most beautiful – most interesting – most days – most careful ______________ is not a superlative[2].

[1] comparative – *erste Steigerungsform des Adjektivs;* [2] superlative – *zweite Steigerungsform*

D5 What animal is best at hitting a baseball?

A bat!

A1 Carnival costumes

a) Look at the photos. What are the costumes? Talk to a partner.

"I think Number 2 is a …"

"I think so, too. And number 5 is a …"

Tipp
Benutze ein Wörterbuch.

b) Compare your ideas with other pairs' ideas and give reasons.

"We think that number 11 is …"

"That's possible. But it could also be …"

"We don't agree. It looks more like …"

c) Which costume do you like most? Describe it in your exercise book.

d) ☆ Do you like celebrating carnival like the people in the photos? Why or why not? Make notes on your ideas. Then give a two-minute talk in class.

portfolio
I can talk

☼ Why do a lot of people like dressing up and celebrating carnival? With a partner, collect ideas. Then give a three-minute talk in class.

A2 ● Carnival here and there

a) Here are two texts in one. Unscramble the texts and mark them in two different colours.

Over 50,000 people take part in it, and there are about 1.5 million visitors each year in August.

In cities such as Cologne, Aachen and Mainz there are big parades and parties.

The festival is also famous for the delicious Caribbean food you can buy there.

In southern Germany, groups of people with wooden masks walk through the towns.

Germans usually celebrate carnival seven weeks before Easter.

It began as a small street party, but now it is one of the biggest parades in Europe.

People wear costumes, dance, sing and have fun, sometimes even at work and at school.

The steel bands usually play the traditional Calypso music.

They often call it the "fifth season".

Immigrants from the Caribbean created Notting Hill Carnival in 1959.

You can see many dancers, singers and steel bands on floats, all of them in bright costumes.

Celebrations take place all over the country, but they are quite different from region to region.

b) Write the texts into your exercise book. Find a good order for the sentences and good titles, too.

A3 ● A crossword

a) Read the sentences and fill in the words.

1. In many places carnival is a big street …
2. A … is a large, decorated car.
3. The Grand Carnival Costume Splash, the Children's Day Parade and all the music performances are … at Notting Hill Carnival.
4. … is a loud sound.
5. Girls and women are … individuals.
6. In a … many people move through the streets, often with bands.
7. Notting Hill Carnival is a … of Caribbean culture.
8. People dress up in … when they go to the carnival.
9. Boys and men are … individuals.

wordbank
festivals

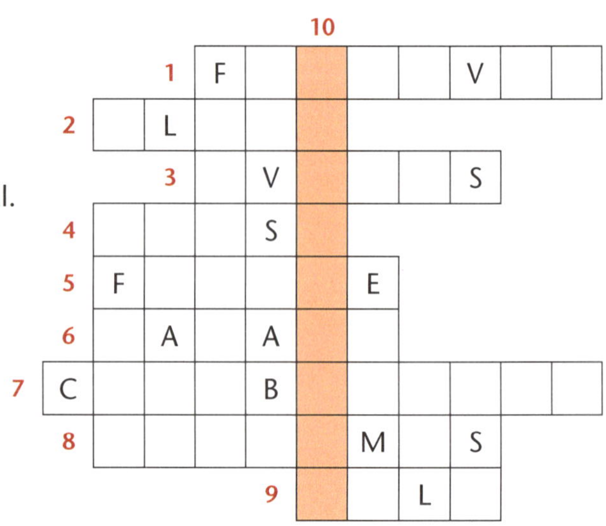

b) Write a sentence for number 10 in which you explain the word.

A4 ● A good day for Rajiv

Make one sentence from two. Use "who", "which" and "that".

1. Rajiv loves watching the crowds of people. The people take part in the carnival parade.

   Rajiv loves watching the crowds of people who take part in the carnival parade.

2. At the last carnival he put up a sign. The sign said: "Buy the best samosas in Notting Hill here."

   ____

   ____

LiF 8

3. He sold his samosas behind a stall. The stall was outside his parents' shop.

   ____

4. He didn't have much time to talk to some classmates. Some classmates stopped at his stall.

   ____

   ____

5. Rajiv also offered sausages. The sausages cost £1.50.

   ____

   ____

6. He sold his food to more than 150 people. The people really liked it.

   ____

   ____

A5 ○ What happened to Charlie?

What happened when Rajiv and David saw Charlie at the parade? Look at the pictures and continue the story. Write it in your exercise book.

Tipp
Finde eine gute Überschrift für die Geschichte.

how to …
write, give feedback

b) **Work with a partner. Edit each other's texts.**

portfolio
I can write

A6 Different opinions

Read A5 "My carnival" in your textbook again and match the sentence parts.

A	Jaide thinks	1	two and a half hours.
B	A pickpocket tried to steal	2	the police have a tough job at the carnival.
C	Driving from Bristol to Notting Hill takes	3	full of rubbish on Sunday night.
D	Kathy was	4	the "Ministry of Sound" party.
E	Emma thinks	5	bands playing in front of his window.
F	Tom really enjoyed	6	it is a bad idea to put the carnival in a park.
G	The streets were	7	not good, but better than other public toilets.
H	Amet does not want	8	on holiday from Australia.
I	The toilets were	9	that Notting Hill Carnival is wicked.
J	Sarah and Emma both think	10	Barry's money.

A	B	C	D	E	F	G	H	I	J

Read A5 "My carnival" in your textbook again and answer the questions.

1. Why does Kathy want to go to the Caribbean for a holiday?

____

____

2. What does Martyn say about the toilets at Notting Hill Carnival?

____

____

3. Why does Amet want to put the Notting Hill Carnival in Hyde Park?

____

____

4. Jaide thinks she has a better idea than Amet. What is it?

____

____

5. What can you find out about the police's job from Emma's blog entry?

____

____

____

A7 Do they like the carnival?

a) Listen to a radio show in which four teenagers are talking about the Notting Hill Carnival. Who likes the carnival and who doesn't? Tick the right box.

CD 1/21

how to … listen

portfolio I can listen

	likes the carnival	doesn't like the carnival	reasons
John	☐	☐	
Alice	☐	☐	
Leo	☐	☐	
Nadira	☐	☐	

b) Listen again. Why do the people like the carnival or why don't they? Take notes in the table.

c) Write about one person in your exercise book. Explain why the person likes or doesn't like Notting Hill Carnival. Use your notes from the table.

Write about the four people in your exercise book. Explain why they like or don't like Notting Hill Carnival. Use your notes from the table.

A8 Sound check

CD 1/28

a) Listen to the words on CD and repeat them.

b) Listen again and fill in the grid.

costume	photo	talk
stall	sausage	watch
poster	float	open
August	shop	short
pocket	walk	don'ts

[əʊ]	[ɒ]	[ɔː]
poster	costume	stall

c) Listen to the CD and check your lists.

CD 1/29

A9 Choose

how to … use the Internet, talk, write

1. Work in groups of three. Find out on the Internet how people celebrate carnival in these countries: Belgium, Switzerland and Italy. Prepare a short talk and present it to the class.
2. Work with a partner. Make notes for a dialogue. One of you likes carnival, the other one doesn't. The person who likes carnival tries to convince[1] the other one to go to a parade with him or her. Then act out the dialogue in class.
3. Would you like to go to Notting Hill Carnival? Write a short text in which you say why or why not.

[1] convince – *überzeugen*

A10 Tips for carnival parties

a) Look at the picture and write down tips for carnival parties. Use these words:

music • decorations • invitations • party games • food • costume

b) Write down three tips for a good costume and three tips for good food.

Write down six don'ts for carnival parties.

c) Present your tips to the class. Then, together, make a poster with tips for carnival parties.

A11 Puzzles

a) Read the sentences and fill in the right word: who • which • that

1. A group of people __________ play music: ☐☐☐☐
2. Shoes __________ are good for walking: ☐☐☐☐☐☐☐☐
3. A woman __________ wears a crown: ☐☐☐☐☐
4. A festival __________ takes place in December: ☐☐☐☐☐☐☐☐☐
5. A person __________ travels to another country: ☐☐☐☐☐☐☐
6. Someone __________ is grown-up: ☐☐☐☐☐
7. A thing __________ keeps your food cold: ☐☐☐☐☐☐
8. People __________ steal purses and watches: ☐☐☐☐☐☐☐☐☐☐☐
9. A kind of food __________ is popular in India: ☐☐☐☐☐☐☐

LiF 8

b) Now fill in the answers.

A12 The West Indies

a) Read A11 "A very short history of the West Indies" in your textbook again. Then choose a title for each paragraph from the box or find your own titles.

In captivity[1] • Working for white masters • Freedom from slavery • A new continent • Slaves from Africa • A time to celebrate • America, not India • A hard life • …

how to … read

1st paragraph: ______________________________

2nd paragraph: ______________________________

3rd paragraph: ______________________________

b) Write down three to five keywords from each paragraph.

1st paragraph: ______________________________

2nd paragraph: ______________________________

3rd paragraph: ______________________________

Write a short summary of the text in your exercise book. Use your titles and keywords.

[1] captivity – *Gefangenschaft*

B1 ● What M. Parlemois saw

a) M. Parlemois, a tourist from Chartres in France, visited the Notting Hill Carnival. Look at his "photos" in B1 "A narrow escape" in your textbook. Write down what M. Parlemois can tell the police about the incident with the six-year-old boy.

portfolio
I can write

Well, this morning I went to ______

I ______

Suddenly ______

______

______

______

______

______

______

______

b) Look at the "photos" in B1 in your textbook again. How would you describe the pickpocket? What does he look like? How old is he? What was he wearing at the parade? Write down what you would tell the police.

______

______

______

______

______

portfolio
I can talk

Work with a partner. Make notes for an interview between a police officer and M. Parlemois. Then act out the dialogue.

B2 ● Rules for car drivers

a) Read the newspaper article.

portfolio
I can help out in English

b) An English friend asks you what the article is about. What do you tell him or her? Summarize[1] the most important information in three sentences.

Keine Masken am Steuer

Auch in diesem Jahr wird die Polizei in der Karnevalszeit wieder viele Autofahrer kontrollieren – und zwar nicht nur, um zu prüfen, ob jemand Alkohol getrunken hat. Auch wer hinterm Steuer eine Maske trägt, muss eine Strafe zahlen, und zwar 10 Euro. Der Grund für das Maskenverbot: Beim Autofahren ist es wichtig, dass man gut sehen und hören kann. Bei großen Masken ist das häufig nicht der Fall.

[1] summarize – *zusammenfassen*

B3 The lost girl

CD 1/24

Look at the picture and listen to the dialogue. Then tick the right answers.

1. Why is Amy, the little girl, crying?
   - ☐ She wants some orange juice.
   - ☐ She has lost her brother.
   - ☐ She wants to phone her mum and dad at home.

2. Why does Rajiv call his mother?
   - ☐ He asks her to sell food for him because there are so many people today.
   - ☐ He asks her to phone Amy's parents.
   - ☐ He asks her to take Amy home.

3. Where does Amy live?
   - ☐ In Lancaster Road.
   - ☐ In Lancaster.
   - ☐ In Ladbroke Grove.

Look at the picture and listen to the dialogue. Then answer the questions.

What is the little girl's problem?

Where are Amy's parents?

How does Rajiv help Amy?

B4 The way home

CD 1/25

a) **Which route do Mrs Patel and Amy take? Listen to the CD and draw their route on the map.**

b) **If Mrs Patel and Amy could take the shortest route, how would they go to Amy's place? Describe the shortest route.**

c) **Amy's brother calls his parents and finds out that his sister is back home. He is at the corner of Chepstow and Talbot Road. How can he walk home? Describe his route.**

Tipp
Benutze einen Bleistift.

B5 ● A busy morning

a) It is the first morning of Notting Hill Carnival. The Patels are very busy in their shop. What is everyone doing? Fill in the right verb forms.

carry • sort • bake • fill • write • prepare

LiF 9R

1. Mr Patel ______________________ the fridge in the shop with soft drinks.
2. Mrs Patel ______________________ Indian cakes.
3. Rajiv ______________________ food to his stall in front of the shop.
4. Sheree ______________________ a sign for Rajiv's stall.
5. A young neighbour ______________________ fresh fruit into different baskets.
6. Grandma Patel ______________________ tea and toast for the family's breakfast.

CD 1/31

b) Listen to the CD and check your sentences.

B6 ● The Hip Hop concert

a) Last night there was a Hip Hop concert on Talbot Road. What were the people doing when the picture was taken?

dance • have • cry • move • flirt • play • watch • eat • call

1. The band ______________________ some popular songs.
2. Gillian and Susan ______________________ wildly.
3. David ______________________ some delicious food.
4. The dark-haired boy from Bristol ______________________ with Susan.
5. Charlie and his uncle ______________________ a great time.
6. A lot of people ______________________ to the beat.
7. The policeman ______________________ a pickpocket.
8. Vanessa ______________________ her mum to ask her if she could stay longer.
9. A little boy ______________________ because he wanted to go home.

LiF 10

portfolio I can work with grammar

CD 1/32

b) Listen to the CD and check your sentences.

B7 ● What was happening?

Make sentences and write the story in your exercise book.

Lots of people Everybody The pickpocket M. Parlemois	were already having fun was looking at the costumes was running away was taking photos was eating at a food stall	when	he knocked John under a float. the police arrested him. M. Parlemois came to the parade. he saw the incident in his camera. the pickpocket stole a wallet.

LiF 10

B8 ● At Notting Hill police station

a) There are quite a few pickpockets at Notting Hill Carnival. Listen and write down what two people told the police.

CD 1/33

Woman: *While I* ____________________

LiF 10

Man: *While I* ____________________

b) Look at the pictures and write down what happened to three other people.

1. *While the woman* ____________________
2. *While* ____________________
3. ____________________

c) Put in "when" or "while".

1. __________ Charlie's uncle was buying some food, someone tried to steal his sunglasses.
2. A girl was laughing about some funny dancers __________ a boy took away her MP3 player.
3. A pickpocket was watching some tourists __________ he noticed a policeman and ran away.
4. __________ Mrs Parker was waiting for the bus, a man snatched[1] her video camera.

[1] snatch – *schnappen*

B9 ○ Choose

how to … talk

1. **Play in a group. One pupil mimes[2] what he or she was doing at some time in the past. Then he or she asks the others: "What was I doing at eight o'clock last Saturday night/ at four o'clock yesterday afternoon/at 7 o'clock this morning/…?" The others have to guess. Examples: "You were watching TV/… playing football/… brushing your teeth."**
2. **Find a photo with many people in it, for example a photo of a school party, a street festival or a celebration in your family. Show the photo to a partner and describe what the different people were doing when the event took place.**
3. **Work with a partner. Compare what you were doing**
   • at 9 pm last Friday • at 10 am last Saturday • at 1 pm last Sunday
   Then tell the class.

[2] mime – *pantomimisch darstellen*

D1 Unscramble the carnival words.

nabd	______	drowc	______
atlof	______	grines	______
darape	______	trayp	______
tesmocu	______	teles rmud	______

D2 Say these sentences as quickly as possible.

Sheree's brother is selling spicy samosas in the street.

Peter Pritchett picks pockets and purses.

Daisy Dickins dresses up and dances with Dave Donalds.

D3 Who or what is it? Find the answers in Theme 3 in your textbook.

1. A man who is wearing dark sunglasses: ______
2. A man who is standing in front of a door: ______
3. A child who is wearing a yellow flower costume: ______
4. A sound system which plays Club Classics and US House: ______
5. Two boys who are playing cards: ______
6. An event that takes place on August 30th from 9 am to 9 pm: ______

D4 What's wrong with these tips for the carnival? Correct them.

1. Bring a lot of money with you so you can buy anything you like.

______

2. Wear high heels[1] so you look hip.

______

3. Stand near the floats so you can get a good look.

______

4. Bring your mobile phone so you can call your friends and tell them about the parade.

______

5. Take the car so you can go home fast after the parade.

______

[1] high heels – *hohe Absätze*

A1 Robinson's adventures

a) Look at A1 "Robinson Crusoe" in your textbook again. Draw a grid like this in your exercise book and take notes on the story.

Who is in the story?	What happens?	Why does it happen?	When and where does it happen?
Robinson Crusoe ...			

A2 What a story!

a) Look at A1 "Robinson Crusoe" in your textbook again. Why is it an adventure story? Tick your answers.

- ☐ Robinson is a brave[1] hero.
- ☐ He is a normal person.
- ☐ The story takes place in a far-away country.
- ☐ Not much happens in the story, but you learn a lot about nature and animals.
- ☐ Robinson is in lots of very dangerous and difficult situations.
- ☐ He has been in many dangerous situations before he is stranded on the island.
- ☐ Everything on the island is unknown to him and he learns how to help himself.

b) Talk to a partner about your ideas. Give reasons for your answers.

portfolio
I can talk

I think *Robinson Crusoe* is an adventure story because ...

I agree.

I don't think so because ...

[1] brave – *tapfer, mutig*

A3 Your talk

how to ...
talk

a) Give a talk about the story of Robinson Crusoe.

- Say who wrote the story.
- Summarize the action. Use your notes from A1.
- Explain why it is an adventure story. Use your ideas from A2.
- Say what you like and don't like about the story.

Tipp
Benutze für deine Geschichte die einfache Gegenwart.

b) Listen to your classmates' talks. After each talk take some notes. Then tell the speakers ...

- what you liked about their talk.
- how they presented the information.
- if they spoke loudly and clearly.
- what they could do better in their next talk. Say this nicely!

portfolio
I can talk

A4 ● Sound check

CD 1/36

a) Listen to the simple past forms and repeat them.
b) Listen again and tick the correct sound.

	[t]	[ɪd]	[d]		[t]	[ɪd]	[d]		[t]	[ɪd]	[d]
tasted	○	○	○	changed	○	○	○	rescued	○	○	○
liked	○	○	○	talked	○	○	○	wanted	○	○	○
loved	○	○	○	worked	○	○	○	asked	○	○	○
boarded	○	○	○	collected	○	○	○	sailed	○	○	○

CD 1/37

c) Listen to the CD and check your answers.

A5 ● Life on the island

a) Fill in the verbs in the simple past.

drink • talk • kill • have • teach • be • watch • begin • call • feel • make • build • live • rescue • cook • go • eat • have • spend

LiF 11R

portfolio I can work with grammar

Robinson ______________ a new life on an island called San Fernandez. He ______________ there for many years. He ______________ bananas and potatoes and he ______________ water and milk. He ______________ animals with a gun and ______________ them on a fire. He ______________ the fire with two stones and dry sticks. So he always ______________ enough food and ______________ his own master. He also ______________ some useful things, for example a raft. For many years, Robinson ______________ no-one to talk to, but he often ______________ to God. Then one day he ______________ a group of cannibals on the beach and he ______________ one of their prisoners. He ______________ him Man Friday. From then on, the two men ______________ a lot of time together. They often ______________ fishing. Robinson ______________ Man Friday how to speak English. He ______________ very happy not to be alone anymore.

CD 1/38

b) Listen to the CD and check your text.

c) Look at the verb forms in the text. Mark the regular and the irregular simple past forms in different colours.

d) Fill in the infinitives of two regular and two irregular verbs. Then swap[1] books with a partner. He or she has to fill in the simple past forms.

Tipp
Trage Verben ein, die auf dieser Seite nicht zu finden sind.

regular verbs		irregular verbs	
infinitive	**simple past**	**infinitive**	**simple past**

[1] swap – *tauschen*

A6 ● Questions for Man Friday

a) People also had lots of questions for Man Friday. Here are some. Unscramble them.

1. cannibals – did – Why – you – the – catch? ______
2. you – Robinson – How – rescue – did – ? ______
3. afraid – Robinson – Were – of – you – ? ______
4. call – Why – Man – you – Robinson – Friday – did – ? ______
______
5. on – like – island – Did – living – the – you – ? ______
6. English – first – were – words – What – your – ? ______
7. celebrate – you – together – Did – Christmas – ? ______
8. did – island – not – Why – stay – the – on – you ? ______

LiF 11R, 12

portfolio I can work with grammar

b) Listen to the CD and check your questions.

CD 1/40

c) Find the answers to the questions. Write the right sentence numbers from a) next to the speech bubbles.

☐ "Please" and "thank you".

☐ Yes, I was at first. But Robinson was really nice to me. So I lost my fear.

☐ Yes, we did. I became a Christian and Robinson told me everything about the festival.

☐ Yes, I did. It was a beautiful place.

☐ They wanted to kill me and eat me.

☐ He fired at the cannibals with his gun.

☐ Because he met me on a Friday.

☐ Robinson wanted to go home and I didn't want to stay alone on the island.

Write down questions that go with these answers.

1. ______ I taught him how to fish for example.
2. ______ Because he was wounded.
3. ______ On 19th December 1686.
4. ______

No, I didn't. It was so cold here and everyone stared at[1] me.

With a partner, write down more questions for Man Friday and find good answers. Read out your dialogues in class.

[1]stare at – *anstarren*

A7 Choose

1. Write down the story from Man Friday's point of view.
2. Write a diary entry for Man Friday. Write about your life in England and your plans for the future. What do you like about England? What don't you like? Do you want to stay with Robinson, live on your own or go back home? If you stay in England, what do you want to do?
3. One night, Robinson and Man Friday are having dinner together and start talking about their life on the island. Work with a partner. Make notes for a dialogue and practise it. Then act it out in class.

A8 Lost at sea

how to ... write, give feedback

Look at the pictures. They show the beginning of an adventure story. You are one of the teenagers in the boat. Write your story.

a) Plan your story first. Make a draft.

WHO?	WHERE?	WHAT?	WHEN?
I my friend / brother / sister ...	at the seaside at sea on a beach/ on an island ...	weather boat water ...	last month / ... two years ago last summer ...

portfolio I can write

b) Write the story.

Last summer I was at the seaside with ...
The weather was ... and we ... Suddenly ...

c) Edit your story:
- Check your words. Use a dictionary.
- Check your verb forms.
- Check if your story is interesting for others to listen to or to read.
- Work with a partner. Edit each other's texts.

portfolio dossier

d) Publish your story. Read it out in class. You can also publish it in your school magazine or on your school's website.

A9 A trip to a dream island

CD 1/31 1/41

a) Be very quiet. Close your eyes and listen.

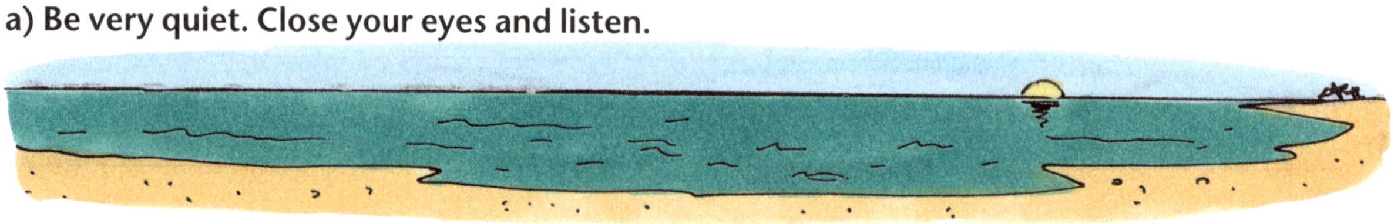

b) Now you have time to write about your trip to the dream island.

A10 ● Holiday on a German island

A British family want to spend their holidays on a German island. They found this information about Spiekeroog, but they don't speak German.

how to ... help out in English

Nordseeinsel SPIEKEROOG

Spiekeroog liegt nahe genug am Festland, um schnell erreichbar zu sein. Und fern genug, um den Alltag hinter sich zu lassen. Himmlische Ruhe bei Tag und bei Nacht. Dünen mit herrlichen Reit- und Wanderwegen – und dahinter der weite Strand.

Die Natur ist Spiekeroogs Schatz und Schutz. Seit 1986 gehört unsere Insel zum Nationalpark Niedersächsisches Wattenmeer, und wir gehen sorgsam mit ihr um. Das bedeutet vor allem: keine Autos! Bei uns fährt man Fahrrad oder geht gleich zu Fuß. Ohnehin sind die meisten Ziele bequem zu Fuß zu erreichen.

Spiekeroog bietet Ferienspaß für die ganze Familie: Sport, Wellness, Ausstellungen, Konzerte und zahlreiche Aktivitäten für Kinder. Und wenn die Sonne mal nicht scheint, lohnt sich ein Besuch im Insel- oder im Muschelmuseum.

Unterkunft
Auf Spiekeroog gibt es keine riesigen Ferienanlagen, aber genug weiche Betten in hübschen Hotels, Pensionen, Ferienhäusern und Ferienwohnungen. In unserer Vermieterdatenbank finden auch Sie die passende Unterkunft. Buchen Sie unter www.spiekeroog-vermieter.de/de/gastgeber.htm.

Anreise
Fährverbindungen ab Neuharlingersiel. Aktuelle Fährpläne und Buchungen unter www.spiekeroog.de.

Answer these questions:
- What is special about Spiekeroog?
- What can you do there?
- How can we book a holiday?
- How can we get there?

Summarize the most important information in five or six sentences.

portfolio
I can help out in English

A11 ○ Choose

how to ... talk

1. **When are you very happy to be at home? What do you do then? Why do you like these times? Make notes and give a talk in class.**

2. **With a partner, collect sayings[1] about "home" from different countries. Make a collage with them. Look up new words so you can explain the sayings in class. Add photos or draw pictures.**
3. **Interview classmates, friends and family members. What does the word "home" mean to them? Take notes. Then present the most interesting answers in class.**

[1] saying – *Sprichwort*

B1 ● Problems

a) What are the teenagers saying about their problems? Use the ideas in the boxes.

terrible at maths • not understand

want to stay at disco until it closes • dad: no, too young

want green hair • dad says: looks stupid

mum says: tidy room • too much work

face: terrible • use lots of different creams

not enough pocket money • not fair

My face

I'm

b) Give answers to the problems in a). Use the phrases from the boxes.

I would … • why don't you …? • I think you should … • you could … • have you tried …?

get a Saturday job • try different colour first • ask teacher for help • put things away after using them • not wear make-up and only wash face with water • talk to dad

Sally,

Patrick,

B2 Hard times, good times

a) What do you do when you have problems? Complete the sentences. You can use ideas from the box or your own ideas.

stay in my room • run for two hours • hide somewhere • listen to sad music • cry • eat a lot of sweets • …

When I feel sad I want to ______

When I'm angry I would like to ______

When I feel shy I would love to ______

When I'm down ______

When I feel lonely ______

When I'm frightened ______

When I feel unhappy ______

LiF 13

wordbank feelings

portfolio I can work with words

b) In your exercise book, write sentences about times when you feel good, happy, great, excited and wonderful.

Write about three different situations in which you felt great. Why did you feel that way? What did you do?

B3 Girls' talk

a) Susan and Gillian are looking at the problem page that you can find in B1 "Letters to Sarah" in your textbook. Listen to the CD. Number the headlines in the order the girls are talking about them.

CD 1/34

Text bullying ☐ My love is a secret ☐ My mum gets on my nerves ☐

I'm so shy ☐ I hate my sister ☐ Dad says: no dog ☐

portfolio I can listen

b) Listen again. Then tick right or wrong.

	right	wrong
1. Gillian always reads the problem page first.	☐	☐
2. Gillian thinks it is a good idea for "Secret from London" to run away with her boyfriend.	☐	☐
3. Susan is glad she has got a cat.	☐	☐
4. Sam Williams always goes blue in the face when he sees Gillian.	☐	☐
5. A girl called Penny had the same problem as "Desperate from London".	☐	☐
6. Gillian and Susan started an action campaign against bullying at their school.	☐	☐
7. Susan says that Rita drives her crazy, but she doesn't hate her.	☐	☐
8. Gillian would like to have a sister.	☐	☐
9. Gillian doesn't get along well with her mum because they never have fun.	☐	☐

c) Correct the wrong sentences. Write the new sentences in your exercise book.

portfolio I can listen

B4 More letters to Sarah

Tipp
Wenn du Hilfe brauchst, schau dir die Briefe im Textbook an.

a) Look at these notes for two letters to Sarah. Choose one problem and write the letter in your exercise book.

problem: bullying
older boy – boss of a group – takes bus money
every morning – group of boys waiting
say mean things, will beat me up
feel desperate

problem: mobile
talk, text messages, photos, music
fun – friends
mum: angry – expensive – take away
can't live without

portfolio
I can learn English

Look at these notes for two letters to Sarah. Choose one problem and write the letter in your exercise book.

problem: computer
big brother – not get off computer
play online computer games – some really bad
not go outside – no sports – never meet friends – not do homework
sometimes: pretend to be ill – not go to school
no weekend activities with family
computer: in his room
parents: not know
really worried

problem: love
in love with boy at school – cute – great basketball player – Ethan
tell best friend, Nicola
plan: Nicola: talk to him about me
now: Ethan & Nicola going out together
Ethan: give her pretty necklace
not want to sit next to her in class
how tell her about my feelings?
disappointed and angry

portfolio
dossier

b) Hang up all your letters in class. Read what your classmates have written.

portfolio
I can write

c) Choose one classmate's letter. First make notes for an answer and then write it.

B5 The Batsons

Read B3 "Meet Charlie's family" in your textbook again.

Now read this text and cross out the wrong words. Then correct the text.

Mr Batson checks magazines and searches the Internet for cars because he is out of work at the moment. He is an engine driver. Every day he walks down to the job centre. Mrs Batson works in a superstore. First she has to fill boxes and then she sits at the information desk. Her boss is nice and makes life easy for her. Josephine is a doctor at St Mary's Hospital in Paddington. She has a 14-hour shift. Her boyfriend has a fast motorbike. Sharon is 12 and often tidies her room. She'd love to go back to hip hop lessons but they are too expensive. Charlie loves playing hockey. He thinks about Susan all the time. His school report was really good.

Answer these questions in your exercise book. Write more than one sentence.

1. What does Mr Batson do to find a new job?
2. Why is it hard for Mrs Batson to work at the supermarket?
3. What is Josephine's life like?
4. What does Sharon like and what doesn't she like?
5. What is important for Charlie?

B6 ● Would you love it or hate it?

What can you say in these situations? Use these phrases:

I'd like to • I'd love to • I'd hate to • I'd rather

1. You very much want to have an ice cream.

I'd love to have an ice cream. ______

LiF 13

2. Your friend has the idea to go to the cinema, but you think it is better to go to the pool.

I'd ______

portfolio
I can work with grammar

3. A foreign student tells you that they have to write twelve maths tests each school year. You think that is terrible.

______

4. You are tired and you dream of lying on a beautiful tropical beach.

______

5. You have to give a talk in science, but you wish you could give a talk in history.

______

B7 ○ Free time activities

a) What do your family and friends do in their free time? Where and when do they do things? Make notes like this on six people's activities:

sister – hip hop class – gym – Fridays

who?	what?	where?	when?

LiF 12

b) Tell your partner about your list.

My sister goes to a hip hop class at a gym on Fridays.

portfolio
I can talk

B8 Always busy

Find out more about Mrs Batson. Which sentence parts do these questions match? Underline the sentence parts and write the questions in the right places.

Why does she hate her job?

When does Mrs Batson get up?

How long does she work?

LiF 12

What does she do when she gets home?

Where does she walk after breakfast?

Mrs Batson gets up at 6 o'clock every day. After a quick breakfast she walks to the supermarket. It is not far away from the Batsons' home. Mrs Batson hates her job because her boss is very unfriendly and the work is hard. She works for 8.5 hours until half past three. When she gets home she does some housework.

When

Find out more about Josephine's day. Make questions about the red sentence parts. Use "who", "what", "when", "where" and "why".

Josephine usually takes the underground to work because the hospital is very far from Hendon. She buys a newspaper on the way to the station. On sunny days she eats her lunch in a little park. St Mary's Hospital is in Paddington. Sometimes her boyfriend takes her to work in his fast car.

B9 Choose

1. Bring a German magazine for teenagers to class. Show the problem page and tell your classmates what the letters are about.
2. A lot of singers and bands sing about problems. Bring one song to class, play it and say what it is about. It can be a German or an English song.
3. Have you seen a film or read a book about teenagers' problems? Give a short talk in class about the film or the book you have chosen. Who are the characters? What are their problems? Why do you like the story?

D1 Put these words together. Sometimes more than one combination is possible.

board	home
catch	a fire
start	a wild animal
point to	alone
leave	a ship
kill	adventures
have	on an island
live	things
collect	a new life

____

____

____

____

____

____

D2 Unscramble these words. They all have to do with Robinson Crusoe's story.

berbiCana | sadlin | kercw | banalcins | ensipror

________ ________ ________ ________ ________

D3 a) Who is it?

She does not like cleaning her room. She can't do her hobby because it is too expensive. That's ______________

He lives in a place where people have to work very hard. But it is the most beautiful place in the world for him. That's ______________

She wants to live on an island with a big waterfall. She would use the waterfall as a shower. That's ______________

He forgets everything when teachers ask him questions. And he does not know how to answer girls. That's ______________

b) Describe two other people in the Theme. Your partner must guess who they are.

D4 Collect words for problems.

____

____

____

D5 A joke

Two frogs sat on Robinson Crusoe's back. One said to the other: "I have to go now . But let's meet again on Friday!"

A1 ● On the train

CD 1/38 2/1

Tipp
Schließe dein Textbook beim Hören.

Listen to A1 "Going up north" in your textbook again. Tick the right answer.

1. David and Gillian are going to spend
   - ☐ the week in Manchester. ☐ the day in Manchester.
   - ☐ the weekend in Manchester.
2. Gillian says that in Manchester there are
   - ☐ lots of cool places. ☐ lots of cool museums. ☐ lots of shops and places to go.
3. Uncle George sent David ☐ a flyer. ☐ a ticket. ☐ a book.
4. The woman says that her favourite place in the Museum of Science and Industry is
   - ☐ the cotton mill. ☐ the Power Hall. ☐ the noisy hall.
5. David's uncle wants to know if the children had
   - ☐ fun on the train. ☐ a good time on the train. ☐ a good journey.

Read these questions. Then listen to A1 "Going up north" in your textbook again and answer the questions.

1. What did Gillian find out about Manchester on the Internet?

   ____

2. Why is it good that David can go to the Museum of Science and Industry?

   ____

3. What does the woman say about the Power Hall in the museum?

   ____

4. Why is Gillian surprised when she hears the on-train announcement?

   ____

5. How long does it take to walk from the station to the museum?

   ____

A2 ○ A free weekend

a) Imagine you have a free weekend and can do whatever you want.

go to • invite • eat • watch • buy • ...

In your exercise book, write down where you would go and what you would do. Say why.

In your exercise book, write down where you would go, what the places are like and what you would do there. Also say why you would go there.

I'd first ... *Then I'd ...* *Next I'd ...*

b) Compare your ideas in class.

A3 ● Useful inventions

a) Write three or four sentences about each of these inventions.

portfolio
I can write

This is a __________ . You can __________

b) Describe another invention but don't say what it is. Read out your text to your partner. He or she must say what it is.

A4 ○ What you need and don't need

a) Fill in the grid. Write at least four inventions in each field.

Inventions …	
I use or need every day	
I often use or need	
I sometimes use or need	
I never use or need	

Tipp
Du kannst ein Wörterbuch benutzen.

wordbank
science

b) Talk to a partner about your grid. Say how often you use or need things and why.

I use my computer every day because I play games on it.

I sometimes need medicine when I'm ill.

A5 Visiting a German museum

You want to take an English friend to the Deutsches Technikmuseum in Berlin.

how to ... help out in English

portfolio I can help out in English

Das Deutsche Technikmuseum lädt Sie zu einer erlebnisreichen Entdeckungsreise durch die Geschichte der Technik ein. Derzeit präsentieren 14 Abteilungen auf rund 25.000 qm Ausstellungsfläche ihre Schätze. Hier erwarten Sie der erste Computer der Welt, zahlreiche Radios, Foto- und Filmkameras, zischende Dieselmotoren und Dampfmaschinen, wissenschaftliche Instrumente, Papiermaschinen und vieles andere mehr.

Tauchen Sie ein in die Ausstellung „Lebenswelt Schiff", oder lassen Sie sich von 40 Eisenbahnen in Originalgröße in den historischen Lokschuppen faszinieren. Erkunden Sie den weitläufigen Museumspark oder träumen Sie vom Fliegen: Die Ausstellung „Vom Ballon zur Luftbrücke" zeigt auf 6.000 qm wesentliche Entwicklungen aus rund 200 Jahren deutscher Luftfahrtgeschichte.

Mit täglichen Vorführungen, Besucheraktivitäten, Führungen und Sonderausstellungen ist das Deutsche Technikmuseum ein spannender Lern- und Erlebnisort. Bei all unseren Angeboten geht es immer um die Fragen: Was für eine Erfindung ist das? Wie wurde sie hergestellt? Wofür wurde sie gebraucht? Hat sie die Welt verändert? Was bedeutet sie für mich? Oder für jemand anderen? Die Besucherinnen und Besucher können schauen, hören und manchmal tasten, Fragen stellen, diskutieren und gemeinsam Antworten suchen. Eine umfangreiche Bibliothek ergänzt das Angebot.

Deutsches Technikmuseum
Trebbiner Straße 9
10963 Berlin-Kreuzberg

Öffnungszeiten
Dienstag bis Freitag: 9.00 – 17.30 Uhr
Samstag / Sonntag: 10.00 – 18.00 Uhr
Montag: geschlossen

Eintrittspreise

	Normal	Ermäßigt
Eintritt	€4,50	€2,50
Gruppen (ab 10 Personen)	€3	€1,50
FamilienPassinhaber*	€3	€1,50

Ab 1. Februar 2009 haben Kinder und Jugendliche bis 18 Jahre ab 15 Uhr freien Eintritt!

* Der FamilienPass ist für €6 im Museumsshop erhältlich.

Tipp
Schau dir im Textbook noch einmal A2 und People&places 4 an.

Look at the flyer and answer your friend's questions:

- Where is the museum?
- What can you see there?
- What are the opening times?
- How much does it cost for us?

Work with a partner. He or she plays the role of your English friend and asks you questions about the museum. Answer them. Then swap roles.

A6 ● Sound check

a) What are these words for inventions you use every day? Write down their names.

'təʊstə	'dɪʃwɒʃə	'reɪdiəʊ	'wɒʃɪŋ mə'ʃiːn	məʊbaɪl'fəʊn
______	______	______	______	______

portfolio
I can learn English

b) Listen to the CD and check your words. c) Check your spelling.

CD 2/2

A7 ○ Easy solutions

What do the people have to do? Use these verbs:

clean • buy • repair • switch off • press • take to • …

The boy has to ______

LiF 14

A8 ● What Robinson had to do

Robinson Crusoe's life was quite difficult. First write down which things he didn't have. Then write down what he had to do.

portfolio
I can write, I can work with grammar

Robinson didn't have a microwave[1], so he had to ______

LiF 14

[1] microwave – *Mikrowelle*

CD 2/2

A9 ● When Grandma Patel was young

a) Rajiv asks his grandmother about life in India when she was young. Listen to the CD and take notes in the table.

portfolio
I can listen

what the family had to do	why?

LiF 14

b) In your exercise book, write sentences with the information in your table.
Grandma Patel's family had to … because … They had to … because …

A10 ○ Choose

portfolio
I can talk

Ask your grandparents or neighbours about life 50 years ago. What things did they have? What didn't they have? What was their life like? Take notes.

1. Give a talk about the most interesting facts.
2. Write a page for a diary about a normal day in the life of a person who lived 50 years ago.
3. With a partner, make notes for a dialogue between two people 50 years ago. They are talking about all the things they have to do that day. Then act out your dialogue.

A11 ○ The talking computer

a) It is Friday evening. Geena and Jeremy Davis are alone at home. Their parents have gone out. What happens? Look at the pictures and make notes on a piece of paper.

how to …
write, give feedback

portfolio
I can write

b) Use your notes to write the story.

c) Work with a partner. Edit each other's texts.

B1 ● A day at MOSI

Read B1 "An amazing day out" in your textbook again. Then close the book and complete the story.

☆ Gillian and David had a great day at the Manchester M_____________ of Science and Industry. First they went to the P_________ Hall and looked at some old m____________. It was very n________ in there. Then they went o___________. They had a r_________ on an old steam l_______________. In the Communications Section David really liked an old c______________ from 1948 called "Baby". In the Main B_____________ the two friends did some e________________. They also went down in an old Manchester s___________. But they did not have t_________ for the Air and Space S_______________, so they want to go to the museum again very soon.

portfolio
I can read

☼ Last weekend Gillian and David went to Manchester. They spent the day at the Museum of _____________ and Industry. First they visited the Power ____________. They looked at engines and _____________ from the old cotton ____________ of Manchester. Then they wanted to get some fresh ___________. So they went outside and had a ___________ on an old steam ______________. It started from the ________ railway station in the _____________. After lunch they looked round the Communications ________________. There they saw a huge, old _________________ from 1948 called "Baby". The Xperiment Section in the _____________ Building was also good _____________. The best thing for David was to go _______________ in an old Manchester ___________. The two friends did not have _________ for the Air and Space _____________, so they decided to go to Manchester again very soon.

B2 ○ Words that go together

a) Match the words from the boxes. Look at B1 "An amazing day out" in your textbook again for help.

get • do • have

experiments • some fresh air • time • a ride • a look round • an idea • a great day

have a great day, have

____

____

____

b) Choose six examples and make sentences with them. Write them in your exercise book.

c) Find more phrases that you often use with the three verbs.

B3 ● Where are they made?

Write down where these things are made and what they are made of.

LiF 15

This snow globe
is made in Germany.
It is made of glass.
____

These Babushkas
are made
____
____

portfolio
I can work with grammar

____
____
____
____

____
____
____
____

~~Germany, glass~~ • Russia, wood • Japan, paper • China, metal

how to ... use the Internet

Find out what these things are made of.

- pencils
- jeans
- CDs
- perfume
- skateboards

Tell the class and explain new words.

B4 ● Interesting, isn't it?

sent • invented • called • created • made • used • designed • sold • opened

a) Fill in the words from the box.

LiF 15

portfolio
I can learn English

1. The telephone was ____________ by Alexander Graham Bell.
2. Over 1.2 billion mobile phones were ____________ last year.
3. Around 200 billion e-mails were ____________ each day in the last few years.
4. The London Eye was ____________ to visitors in 2000.
5. The first hot-air balloon was ____________ by the Montgolfier brothers.
6. One of the first computers was ____________ "Baby".
7. The World Wide Web was ____________ in 1990.
8. In the 19th century, steam-powered engines were ____________ in the cotton mills.
9. A lot of clothes are ____________ in Asia.

CD 2/3

b) Listen to the CD and check your sentences.

Look at B3 and B4 again. Complete the sentences to find the rules.

You use ________ / ________ + ____________ to form the passive in the simple present.

You use ________ / ________ + ____________ to form the passive in the simple past.

B5 ● Invented by?

a) Look at the pictures and read the table. Then fill in the words for the inventions.

light bulb

matches

zip

ballpoint pen

CD

stamp

invention	inventor	what for?	when?
	Whitcomb Judson	to help you close your anorak	
	James Russell	to listen to music	
	Thomas Edison	to help you see when it is dark	
	James Chalmer	to put on a letter	
	John Walker	to light a fire	
	Laszlo Biro	to write with	

LiF 15

b) Listen to the CD and fill in the dates under "when?"

CD 2/3

c) Write about the inventions.

The zip was invented in ______ by ______

______

______

______

______

______

Choose one of the inventions in the grid and find out some facts about its history. Give a three-minute talk.

B6 ○ When was it done?

a) Answer the questions.

LiF 15

1. **Your** school: when was it opened? ______
2. **Your** house: when was it built? ______
3. An important building in **your** area (for example a museum or a sports stadium): when was it built/opened? ______
4. A book **you** have read: who was it written by? ______
5. The shirt or pullover **you** are wearing: where was it made? ______

b) Write a short text about an interesting or a famous building. It can be in your home town or far away. Find out when it was built, when it was first used or when it was opened to visitors. Choose the most interesting information.

B7 ● Hit or flop?

Ben Sickness is interviewing Karen Waterman about a very special car.

CD 2/4

Listen to the CD. Then read these sentences. There is one mistake in each sentence. Cross out the wrong words and correct them.

1. The radio programme is for listeners of Radio 13.
2. The programme is called "Out and aloud."
2. Ben says he can do 65kph on his motorbike, too.
3. Karen says that Ben is turning green.
4. On water the wheels work like a rudder[1].
5. When Karen and Ben are back on land, a pump starts pumping the air out of the Amphicar.
6. Karen says Ben should come on a stormy day if he wants to have real fun.

portfolio
I can listen

Listen to to the CD. Then answer these questions in your exercise book.

1. What is the weekly report on Radio 12 called?
2. Where do Ben Sickness and Karen Waterman meet?
3. Ben Sickness can't remember the name of the Amphicar. What does he call it?
4. Why is Ben getting nervous when they come to the lake?
5. How do you steer the Amphicar?
6. Why is there a pump in the Amphicar?
7. Why is Ben happy when they are back on land?

[1] rudder – *Ruder*

B8 ○ Choose

portfolio
I can talk

1. **Draw an Amphicar and label all the parts that you can name.**
2. **Would you like to have an Amphicar? Give a short talk in which you say why or why not.**
3. **Is it better to have a car and a boat or just one Amphicar? Give a short talk in which you explain what you think.**
4. **What is your dream vehicle? Write a text in which you describe it and say why you would like to have it. You can add a photo or a drawing.**

B9 ● Sound check

CD 2/4

a) Listen to the CD and fill in the lists.

Handsome[2] **Harry**'s from the Isle of **Man**.
And he's such a **trendy Amphicar fan**.
He's got a big **catalogue**, he's so lucky,
Sent by **Karen**, his **pen pal** from **Kentucky**.
Harry and Karen are **planning** to **marry**
The **wedding** party will be on an Amphiferry.
Two Amphicar fans on sea and on **land**!
Now won't that be a **happy event**?

[2] handsome – *gutaussehend*

[æ]: handsome, ______

______

______

______

[e]: trendy, ______

______

______

CD 2/5

b) Listen and check your lists.

c) Practise reading the poem aloud. Be careful with [æ] and [e].

B10 ● An exhibition of fantastic firsts

a) Listen to the CD and number the pictures in the right order.

CD 2/5

b) Listen again. What is special about the inventions? Take notes.

c) Which are your two favourite inventions? Describe them and say why you like them.

Describe each invention in detail. Write the texts in your exercise book.

B11 Solar marshmallow cooker

how to … read

a) Look at the title and the pictures. What kind of text is it? Tick the correct answer.

☐ story ☐ instruction ☐ poem

You need: a cardboard box, aluminium foil, some flexible and some stiff cardboard, some tape, a wooden stick, marshmallows

1. Cut the long sides of the cardboard box as in the picture. Your teacher will give you a parabolic curve.
2. Cut out a piece of flexible cardboard. Stick aluminium foil on the cardboard with the shiny side out. Do not wrinkle the foil!
3. Fix the cardboard on the opening of the box with some tape. Start at the centre.
4. Tape two pieces of stiff cardboard to each side of the box as holders.
5. Put marshmallows on a stick. Then put the stick through the holders.

Use your marshmallow cooker in sunny weather around lunchtime. You'll always have a nice dessert!

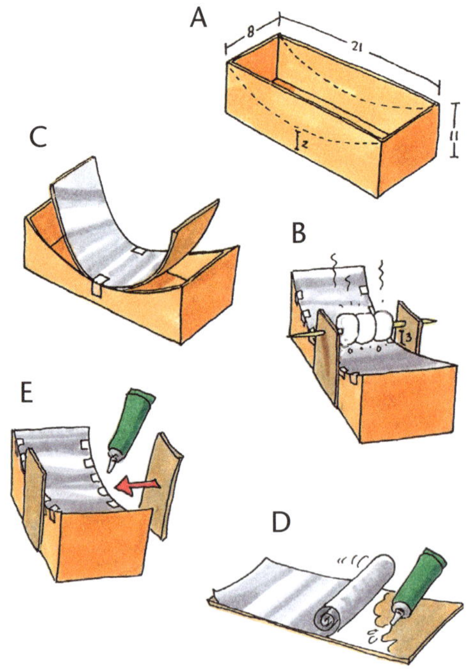

b) Now read the text. Write down the words you don't know. Try the four different ways to find out what they mean. Note down how you found out.

Words I don't know	1 The English word is similar to a German word.	2 Other words helped me.	3 The pictures helped me.	4 I used a dictionary.

c) Match the parts of the text with the pictures (A–E).

1		2		3		4		5	

d) Now make a solar marshmallow cooker. Have fun!

D1 Find the answers in Theme 5 in your textbook.

When did Avro Shackleton design his aeroplane? ______

Who invented the hook and loop fastener? ______

Where is the Centre for Alternative Technology? ______

What is *Planet?* ______

What was one enterprising cyclist's invention? ______

What is the name of the famous football club from Manchester? ______

Where can you lift a Mini car? ______

In which town can you get face to face with Vikings? ______

D2 Read the limerick and learn it by heart.

There was a young lady called Joan
Who was unhappy when she was alone.
Her mother bought Joan
A new mobile phone,
Now she's never alone with her phone.

D3 Odd one out – but why?

1. oven – toaster – dishwasher – wheel – fridge ______
2. invention – adult – visitor – friend – pupil ______
3. see – hear – smell – read – taste ______
4. computer – museum – matches – bicycle – medicine ______
5. cool – super – free – brilliant – wonderful ______

D4 a) Read this list of useless inventions.

a solar-powered torch
a black highlighter pen
fireproof matches
a silent alarm clock
double-sided playing cards

b) With a partner, come up[1] with three more useless inventions.

______

______

______

[1] come up with – *sich etwas einfallen lassen*

A1 ● An interview about pocket money

CD 2/7

Listen to Debbie, Sarah and Anwar on a radio programme for teenagers. What do they say about pocket money?

Underline the correct answers.

	Debbie	Sarah	Anwar
age	12 13 14	12 13 14	13 14 15
pocket money	£10 £14 £12	£10 £8 £13	£13 £15 £12
spends it on	mobile phones magazines make-up	cat food CDs computer magazines	computer games computer magazines CDs
does these jobs to earn pocket money	cleans the bathroom tidies the living room tidies her own room	cooks dinner feeds the dog feeds the cat	doesn't do anything does a few things for his mum does a lot of things for his dad

a) Take notes in the grid.

	Debbie	Sarah	Anwar
age			
pocket money			
spends it on			
does these jobs to earn pocket money			

b) Who thinks that he or she does not get enough pocket money?

A2 ○ Making some extra money

a) Sort your ideas from TB A2 "Short of cash" into the grid.

wordbank
jobs and money

at home	at other people's places	at school
feed the cat	*do the shopping*	*put on a class concert*

b) With a partner, add more ideas.

c) Have you ever done any of the jobs in the grid? If yes, tell the class about it.

I sometimes do the shopping for an old lady.

Last month I tidied the garage for my parents.

Tipp
Du kannst ein Wörterbuch benutzen.

A3 ● What can they do?

a) Read what the children want to have or do. How can they get the money? Write your ideas in your exercise book.

Charlie wants to have some new books about goldfish.
David wants to buy more comics and magazines.
Susan would like to have a new animal poster.
Rajiv wants to save money for a new guitar.
Vanessa would like to have tickets for a pop concert.
Gillian wants to take part in a streetdance workshop.

If Charlie ..., he can buy some new books ...
If Rajiv ..., he will be able to save ...

LiF 16

b) Compare your ideas with a partner's.

A4 ○ At the car boot sale

Read the dialogue in A4 "A car boot sale" in your textbook again. Then underline the wrong words in these sentences. Correct the words.

1. Gillian and Vanessa are going on a holiday to France. _______________
2. They offer a new toaster. _______________
3. Rosemary wants to buy something really special. _______________
4. Rosemary thinks that the picture looks strange. _______________
5. She buys the vase, the picture and a glass pig for £12. _______________
6. Aunt Elsie runs a big antique shop in Kensington Church Street. _______________

Read the dialogue in A4 "A car boot sale" in your textbook again. Then correct these sentences.

portfolio
I can read

1. Mrs Collins was really happy about the girls' idea to sell things at the car boot sale.

____

2. The girls are worried that nothing will be left at the end of the day.

____

3. Rosemary thinks the vase is awful but Gillian and Vanessa find it fantastic.

____

4. Rosemary has seen lots of pictures like the Picasso before.

____

5. Aunt Elsie works in a big antique shop in Kensington Street.

____

6. Rosemary will earn £6 if Aunt Elsie takes the picture and the glass pig.

____

A5 ● What Ruby bought

a) Put in "some" or "any".

LiF 18R

1. My friend Ruby loves car boot sales and she always brings home ________ nice things.
2. She went to a sale yesterday and bought ________ pretty old cups for her mum.
3. She also wanted to buy ________ clothes, but she didn't find ________ that she liked.
4. One seller had Ruby's favourite comics so she got ________ .
5. She thought she would meet ________ friends at the sale.
6. But she didn't see ________ people she knew.
7. So she had ________ tea and biscuits and went home again.

CD 2/12

b) Listen to the CD and check your sentences.

A6 ● A present for David's dad

a) Charlie and his mother are selling some old things at a flea market. Read the dialogue and put in these words.

some | any | something | anything

LiF 17, 18R

portfolio: I can work with grammar

Charlie: Oh Mum, this is so boring. We haven't had ____________ customers yet. Won't we sell ____________ today?

Mrs Batson: It's still early. Most people haven't sold ____________ yet. But look, here's David.

Charlie: Oh hi, David. What are you doing here? Do you want to buy ____________?

David: Hi, Mrs Batson. Hi, Charlie. I need ____________ special for my dad's birthday.

Charlie: Has he got ____________ hobbies?

David: No, not really. He reads a lot but I don't want to buy ____________ books. I'm sure my mum will give him ____________.

Mrs Batson: Hmm, as you can see we've got ____________ toys, ____________ clothes and ____________ kitchen things. But I'm afraid we haven't got ____________ you could give your dad as a present.

David: Too bad. Well, then I'll have a look at ____________ of the other stalls.

Charlie: Wait a second. Didn't you tell me that your dad loves Notting Hill Carnival? Look here. My uncle gave me ____________ steel drums and asked me to sell them. Wouldn't that be ____________?

David: Brilliant idea! Dad could also take drumming classes after work. How much are they?

Charlie: £6 – my special offer for you and you'll have ____________ really unusual.

David: OK, I'll take them. They're very nice.

CD 2/13

b) Listen to the CD and check your dialogue.

A7 Shopping phrases

Listen to the dialogues from A7 "At the flea market" in your textbook again and answer the questions.

CD 2/9

Was sagt man, wenn …

- man sich für eine Hose interessiert? I'm
- man einen Preis angemessen findet? That's

Wie fragt man, …

- wenn man Hilfe braucht? I wonder if
- welchen Preis die Verkäuferin einem anbieten kann? What price
- ob jemand sich etwas genauer ansehen möchte? Would you like
- ob die Verkäuferin ein gutes Angebot machen kann? Can you

A8 Role plays

portfolio
I can talk

Work with a partner and act out the scene.

Partner A: Käufer/Käuferin

1 Du siehst auf dem Flohmarkt mehrere MP3-Player. Frage B, ob sie noch gut funktionieren.
3 Suche einen aus. Frage nach dem Preis.
5 Sage, dass das zu teuer ist, suche einen einen anderen aus und frage, wie viel dieser kostet.
7 Sage, dass du nur £8 hast.
9 Sage, dass du ihn nimmst, und gib B das Geld.
11 Verabschiede dich.

Partner B: Verkäufer/Verkäuferin

2 Antworte A, dass alle MP3-Player noch gut funktionieren.
4 Antworte, dass er £10 kostet.
6 Antworte, dass er ebenfalls £10 kostet, und frage A, wie viel er/sie denn ausgeben möchte.
8 Zeige A einen anderen MP3-Player und sage, dass er/sie ihn für £8 haben kann. Ergänze, dass er auch richtig gut ist.
10 Bedanke dich.
12 Verabschiede dich.

Work with a partner and act out the scene.

Partner A: Käufer/Käuferin

1 Du siehst auf dem Flohmarkt einen Stand mit alten Möbeln und fragst B, ob es echte Antiquitäten sind.
3 Suche einen Stuhl aus und frage nach dem Preis.
5 Sage, dass das zu teuer ist. Dann siehst du eine Vase. Frage, wie viel sie kostet.
7 Sage, dass das auch zu teuer ist.
9 Sage, dass du nur £10 hast.
11 Sage, dass du sie nimmst, und gib B das Geld.
13 Verabschiede dich.

Partner B: Verkäufer/Verkäuferin

2 Antworte A, dass du nur echte Antiquitäten hast.
4 Antworte, dass er £25 kostet.
6 Antworte, dass sie ungefähr 100 Jahre alt ist und £12 kostet. Ergänze, dass dies ein richtiges Schnäppchen ist.
8 Frage A, wie viel er/sie ausgeben möchte.
10 Sage, dass er/sie die Vase für £10 haben kann. Ergänze, dass dies ein Sonderangebot für ihn/sie ist.
12 Bedanke dich.
14 Verabschiede dich.

A9 ● Gillian and Vanessa's ideas

a) Match the sentence parts. Write the correct sentences in your exercise book.

LiF 16

1. If Gillian and Vanessa collect lots of old things,	a. they will be able to go shopping in France.
2. If the weather is good on Saturday,	b. they will be able to make a nice album.
3. If the girls sell enough,	c. lots of people will come to the sale.
4. If they have some pocket money,	d. they will have a great time.
5. If they see nice clothes in French shops,	e. their families will be glad.
6. If they visit lots of different places in France,	f. they will offer them at the car boot sale.
7. If they take lots of photos on the trip,	g. they will buy them.
8. If they bring home souvenirs,	h. they will have some pocket money for the trip.

CD 2/14

b) Listen to the CD and check your sentences.

A10 ● If you have got a Picasso …

Look at the pictures and write sentences with "if".

sell for thousands of pounds

be rich

travel around the world

visit lots of famous places

be in the magazines

get invitations to fantastic parties

meet interesting people

LiF 16

If you have got a Picasso, you can sell it for thousands of pounds.

If you sell it for thousands of pounds, you will __________

If you are __________

____

____

____

____

portfolio
I can work with grammar

A11 ● What if …?

a) Look at these "What if?" questions and write down what you will or won't do.

If my favourite TV star sits next to me on the bus, I will invite her to my birthday party.

What if …

your favourite TV star sits next to you on the bus?
you lose your mobile phone?
they close the school?
your aunt gives you 100 euros?
you can work as a dishwasher in a fast food place?
you design a new computer game?
you come up[1] with a delicious new soft drink?

____

____

____

____

____

____

____

____

____

____

LiF 16

b) On a sheet of paper, write down three "What if?" questions for your partner to answer.

[1] come up with something – *sich etwas ausdenken*

A12 ○ Rags-to-riches stories

a) **Here are some people whose lives have been rags-to-riches stories. Choose one of them and find out more about his or her life on the Internet. Take notes. These questions can help you:**

- How did the person grow up? Why was his or her life hard?
- When did the person become successful and rich? How did it happen?
- What is special about the person? How did he or she make it? What does the person do to stay successful?

b) **Work with a partner who has collected information about the same famous person. Compare your notes. Then choose the most interesting facts and prepare a talk.**

c) **Together give your talk in class.**

Bill Clinton

Céline Dion

J.K. Rowling

Eminem

how to … use the Internet, talk

portfolio I can talk

B1 ● Can you remember?

a) How much do you still know about London? Fill in the names of the sights and places.

The Queen lives here: _ U _ _ _ _ _ H _ ■ _ _ _ _ C _

You can see wax figures here: M ■ D A _ _ _ _ S S _ _ _ S

It opens when large ships pass: _ _ W _ ■ _ _ _ D G _

A place with shops and stalls: _ O V _ _ T G ■ _ D _ _

The Londoners' name for their underground: ■ _ B _

Londoners and tourists come here to relax: ■ Y _ _ P _ _ K

A place where you can see wild animals: _ _ N D _ _ _ ■ _

A place where you can find out about dinosaurs:

■ _ T _ R _ _ _ _ S T _ R Y _ U S _ _ _

b) Fill in the marked letters from a).

An event that takes place each year in April: ■ ■ ■ ■ ■ ■ ■ ■

B2 ● Facts about the race

a) Read B1 "The London Marathon" in your textbook again. Then tick right, wrong or not in the text.

	right	wrong	not in the text
1. There are four races in the London Marathon.			
2. There are four starting points for the 33,000 runners.			
3. The fastest runners are in the Elite Race.			
4. The runners in the Mass Race collect money for every mile they run.			
5. All the runners in the Mass Race dress up.			
6. The Wheelchair Marathon starts at 9.25 from the Grey Start.			
7. A lot of runners from Australia take part in the London Marathon.			
8. The Mini Marathon is for people between the ages of 11 and 17.			
9. The race finishes after 42.195 miles.			
10. The women's world record is 2:03:59.			

portfolio
I can read

b) Correct the wrong sentences. Write the new sentences in your exercise book.

B3 ● Passing lots of sights

CD 2/11

The marathon runners pass lots of sights. Listen to B2b) "Off they go" in your textbook again and find the correct order for the sights. Write numbers from 1 to 10 in the boxes.

☐ Tower Bridge	☐ Canary Wharf Tower
☐ The Houses of Parliament	☐ Woolwich Ferry
☐ St. Katharine's Dock	☐ Buckingham Palace
☐ The Mall	☐ The Tower of London
☐ Cutty Sark	☐ Isle of Dogs

portfolio
I can listen

B4 ○ Charlotte's training plan

a) Charlotte, a girl from London, has written an article for her school magazine about the Mini Marathon. What information does it give about training, food and drink? First underline the sentences you need to fill in the training plan. Then take notes.

how to ... read

portfolio
I can learn English

Preparing for the Mini Marathon

Hi, I'm Charlotte Edmonds. I'm 13 and I'm in year 8. I'm running the Mini Marathon at the London Marathon this year. I did it last year and it went well. But it was difficult to get up every morning at 5.30 am to get the bus on time.
This year it's the same. We train every morning before school. First we do some warm-ups, then run 1.7 miles and after that we do some stretching. I always go to bed early so that I'm not tired. I also eat a lot of healthy food in the weeks before the marathon: a lot of fruit, vegetables and a lot of pasta – not too difficult because pasta is my favourite food! And I drink a lot, too. Everyone should drink at least two litres of water a day, but as a runner you have to drink extra water or a sports drink after training.
It's now only two weeks until the race starts. I'm so excited! See you at the marathon!

Training plan

Training:

____

____

____

Food:

____

____

____

Drink:

____

____

b) Tell someone in German how Charlotte prepares for the Mini Marathon.

portfolio
I can help out English

c) ☆ Work with a partner. One of Charlotte's classmates who has not read the article asks her about her preparations for the Mini Marathon. Make up a dialogue and act it out.

Find information about the Mini Wheelchair Marathon on the Internet. When did it start? Where and when does it take place? Who can take part in it? How do the athletes prepare for the race? Collect important facts and give a talk in class.

how to ... use the Internet

B5 ● Sound check

CD 2/16

a) Listen to the CD and repeat the words.

b) Colour in the words. Use different colours for words with [aɪ] and [eɪ].

change | mile | same | date | life | race | night | sky

April | apply | train | flyer | day | high | age | buying

CD 2/17

c) Listen to the CD again and check your words.

B6 ● Tips for runners

a) Write down useful tips for people who want to be good marathon runners.

can | must

try out different places in town • ask friend to run with you • go to bed early • check route before race • do some warm-up exercises before you start • ~~train every day~~ • eat healthy food

1. If you want to be a successful marathon runner, *you must train every day.*
2. If you want to be fit in the morning, ______
3. If you want to keep your weight, ______
4. If you don't know where to practise, ______
5. If you get bored training on your own, ______
6. If you are nervous before the marathon, ______
7. If you don't want to have sore legs after training, ______

______

LiF 16

portfolio
I can work with grammar

b) Write down at least three special tips for runners in the Mini Marathon. Use if-clauses. You can look at B4 for ideas.

______

______

______

______

______

Add if-clauses to these tips. Write the sentences in your exercise book.

1. If …, you must do some stretching after training.
2. If …, you must drink a lot of water.
3. If …, you can keep a runner's diary.
4. If …, you must buy the right clothing for any kind of weather.
5. If …, you can chat with other runners on the Internet.

B7 ● When will they finish?

Look at these runners and the starting times of the races in B1 "The London Marathon" in your textbook. Write down at what time they will finish their races.

LiF 16

No. 3679
Bertha Jackson
Fun runner
Personal best time: 5:16:25

No. 4168
Felix Reiser
Elite runner
Personal best time: 2:19:40

No. 6546
Jacob Burton
Wheelchair race
Personal best time: 3:03:23

No. 7112
Vikram Bihal
Fun runner
Personal best time: 4:32:02

No. 8444
Samantha Davis
Elite runner
Personal best time: 2:36:51

No. 9164
Alicia Young
Wheelchair race
Personal best time: 2:51:24

If Bertha Jackson does her best time, she will finish at about 3.01 pm.

If Jacob Burton ________________

____

____

____

____

B8 ○ Rajiv's race

a) Rajiv ran in the last Mini Marathon. What happened? Look at the pictures and make notes.

how to … write, give feedback

portfolio I can write

b) Use your notes to write the story.
c) Work with a partner. Edit each other's texts.

B9 About Red Nose Day

CD 2/13

Radio DJ Tom Kingsley is interviewing Elaine Groves. She is one of the people who organized this year's Red Nose Day.

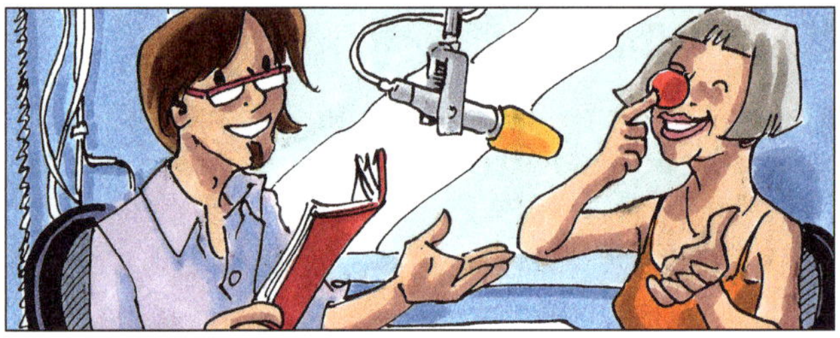

a) Listen to the interview and complete the sentences.

how to ... listen

1. The people who have organized Red Nose Day help poor people in ________________.
2. They build schools and buy ________________.
3. They also have projects in the UK for the ________________ and elderly.
4. Many schools did funny ________________ on Red Nose Day.
5. Some pupils and teachers tried to eat jelly without using their ________________.

b) Do you think that Red Nose Day is a good idea? Why or why not? In your exercise book, write three or four sentences in which you explain your opinion.

a) Listen to the interview. Take notes on these questions.

1. How much money have charities collected since the first Red Nose Day?
2. Which projects get the money?
3. What funny projects does Elaine talk about?

b) Use your notes to write a text about Red Nose Day.

B10 Famous charities

a) Here are some famous charities. With a partner, find out what the letters stand for.

UNICEF | OXFAM | WWF | RSPCA

b) Choose one organization. Use the Internet to fill in this grid.

how to ... use the Internet

organization	
started in/by	
most important projects	
money raised	

Tipp
Achtet darauf, dass eure Redezeit etwa gleich lang ist.

c) With your partner, give a three-minute talk about the organization. Use your grid.

B11 Choose

1. **Work with a partner. Use the Internet to find more information about Red Nose Day. Who started it? What do people do on the day? What is special about the day? When was it started in Germany? Present the information in class.**
2. **Write a text about an organization that helps people or animals. You can use the information from B10.**
3. **Use the Internet to find information about the marathons in one of these cities:**
   - **Berlin**
   - **Chicago**
   - **New York**

   Present the information in class.

D1 Who are the people? What are the things and places?

1. This is a person who gives a runner money. ______________________
2. This is the largest annual fundraising event in the world. ______________________
3. This is more important to runners in the Mass Race than time. ______________________
4. This is a famous old ship that tourists can visit on the River Thames. ______________________
5. This is a famous Spanish painter. ______________________
6. This is a person who got $240 million from Microsoft. ______________________
7. This is a fundraising activity where people don't talk. ______________________
8. These are places where you can win a fortune in a game. ______________________

D2 Read the descriptions of things you can buy at a car boot sale. Fill in the words.

You wear them.	_ _ _ T H _ _
You need it in the rain.	_ _ B _ _ _ _ _
You read stories and articles in them.	_ _ G _ _ _ _ _ _
Children play with them.	T _ _ _
You put flowers in it.	_ _ _ E
You wear it on your arm and it tells you the time.	W _ _ _ _
Somebody painted it.	_ _ C _ _ _ _
You sit on it.	_ _ _ _ R
You put food on it.	_ _ A _ _

Gillian and Vanessa need money for a _ _ _ _ _   _ _ _ _

D3 Who says this?

1. "Picasso? That's a French car, isn't it?" ______________________
2. "I've never seen anything like that before." ______________________
3. "In my dreams I have a plan." ______________________
4. "Someone might by it." ______________________

D4 What's wrong with these people?

A1 What Pink's fans say

a) Read what fans say about Pink. Use different colours to underline what they say about:

- **her music**
- **her character**
- **her ideas**
- **her looks**

portfolio
I can read

I went to a Pink concert in Manchester a few months ago and became one of her greatest fans after that. Her music touches me deeply. She is also a very nice person – open, friendly and very funny. I even decided to get tattooed after I saw her. Pink, you rock, babe!!!!
Alicia from Blackpool

I haven't got a tattoo or pink hair but I just love her music! I sing and write songs, too, and she has been such an inspiration to me. She has also helped me through a lot of hard times just because she sings about herself. I want to thank her for going out there and being who she is. That's why I am now who I am.
Tricia from Chicago

She's tough and in control.
Derek from Melbourne

I love animals and I love Pink because she is a strong supporter of animal rights. What she does for animals is great.
Bob from New York

Pink sings what she thinks, and she has got strong opinions. She is not afraid to speak her mind. Everything she sings is true.
Gabor from Budapest

Pink is so beautiful and I love her fantastic voice. She sings what she really feels. All this makes her very special.
Maria from Madrid

She knows what young people's lives are like. That's why I love her songs.
Sandy from South Africa

She is simply fantastic on stage!
Sven from Oberhausen

I can't get enough of Pink's music and I like her because she is such a special person. She is so generous and gives lots of money to different organizations. For example, she gave $250,000 when there were large fires in Australia. That's great.
Miha from Warsaw

Pink has created her own style. Her hair, her tattoos and her clothes look so cool.
Bernice from Edinburgh

b) In your exercise book, draw a grid like this and take notes in it.

What fans like about Pink's …			
music	character	ideas	looks

c) Work with a partner. Partner A is a Pink fan and Partner B is a fan of another singer. Make up a dialogue. Then act it out in class.

d) ★ Do you want to be like Pink or like another star? Say why or why not.

☼ Do you think that Pink can be a role model[1] for young people? Say why or why not.

[1] role model – *Vorbild*

A2 ○ The future of a star

This is Pink's life now:

She lives in the USA.
She is a musician and an actress.
She has got blond hair.
She likes animals.
She is a strict vegetarian.
She dislikes horror movies.
She loves her tattoos.
She has won two Grammys.

What will her life be like in 10 years' time? Write about it.

I think she will Perhaps she will/won't I don't think she will	live in be have like …	…

A3 ● Joseph and the Amazing Technicolour Dreamcoat

Listen to A4 "Casting shows" in your textbook again.
Tick right oder wrong.

CD 2/14

	right	wrong
1. Lee Mead was chosen by BBC television viewers to play the role of Joseph in the remake[1] of Andrew Lloyd Webber's musical.	☐	☐
2. The show started with 150 contestants[2].	☐	☐
3. Twenty contestants were taken to Andrew Lloyd Webber's castle in Scotland.	☐	☐
4. Each day the "Josephs" were set various singing and performing tasks.	☐	☐
5. Like all casting shows Joseph was a lot of hard work.	☐	☐
6. In the final Lee sang "Somewhere over the rainbow".	☐	☐

Read the sentences and fill in the missing words.

1. Last night the BBC presented the final of the ______________________ .
2. Lee Mead was chosen by ________________ viewers to play the role of __________ in Andrew Lloyd Webber's ______________ *Joseph and the Amazing Technicolour Dreamcoat.*
3. Twenty young men were taken to Andrew Lloyd Webber's castle in ______________________.
4. For the finals the best ____________ were taken to ______________.
5. Like all ______________________ *Joseph* was a lot of hard work.
6. At the end of the __________ it was the viewers' votes that counted.
7. Lee sang "Any ____________ will do." His prize was __________ months in the lead role[3] of *Joseph and the Amazing Technicolour Dreamcoat.*

portfolio
I can listen

[1] remake – *Neuauflage* [2] contestant – *Kandidat/in* [3] lead role – *Hauptrolle*

A4 ● Problems before the gig

Read A6 "Sabrina and the Gatecrashers" in your textbook again.

Match the sentence parts.

A The Gatecrashers have just come back	1 has four days off.
B The group is recording	2 at 3 o'clock.
C Fred has booked the Electric Theatre	3 the Gatecrashers' London Fan Club.
D After the concert the group	4 a new album next month.
E Half of the roadies	5 but at least they have got free tickets.
F Fred has phoned	6 from a very successful concert in Reading.
G Ten kids come to the Electric Theatre	7 at 12 o'clock on Saturday.
H The rehearsal starts	8 for a gig next weekend.
I Gillian and Susan are tired	9 have gone home.

A		B		C		D		E		F		G		H		I	

portfolio
I can read

Answer the questions.

1. How do you know that the Gatecrashers are a successful band?

___

2. Why has Fred booked the Electric Theatre for a gig?

___

3. Why does Sabrina get angry with Fred?

___

4. When can the band get a rest and for how long?

___

5. Half of the roadies have gone home. What has Fred done about that?

___

6. What do the people who help the Gatecrashers get for their work?

___

A5 ○ Choose

1. **Imagine you are Gillian or Susan. Write a blog entry for Sabrina's fan site in which you explain what is special about her. Look at the pictures in A6 "Sabrina and the Gatecrashers" in your textbook and at A1 in this workbook again.**
2. **Work with a partner. Make up the phone call between Fred and a person at the Gatecrashers' London Fan Club in which Fred asks for help before the gig. Act out the dialogue in class.**
3. **Write a diary entry for Sabrina the week after the concert.**

A6 ● Tell us, Sabrina …

a) After the concert the fans have got lots of questions for Sabrina. Find the answers to the questions. Write down the right numbers.

A When do you get up in the morning?

B Is it true that Hank is your boyfriend?

C When is your birthday?

D Do you like sports?

E Can you cook?

F Where do you want to live when you are grown up?

1 No, he isn't. He's just a good friend.

2 I often jog in the park in the late afternoon.

3 On a sunny island.

4 I can make spaghetti with meat sauce.

5 I usually get up at 7 o'clock during the week.

6 It's on 5th July.

LiF 19

A		B		C		D		E		F	

b) Write down in your exercise book what Sabrina says.

Sabrina tells the girl with the orange T-shirt that she usually gets up at 7o'clock during the week.

A7 ○ Interviews

a) Ask your partner and tick his or her answers.

Questions for ______________________	yes	no
Is Pink a good singer?	☐	☐
Is band manager an interesting job?	☐	☐
Are concert tickets too expensive?	☐	☐
Is it bad for children and teenagers to become stars?	☐	☐
Should pop stars sing about problems?	☐	☐

LiF 19

b) Report to the class what your partner thinks.

… thinks that Pink is a good singer.

… thinks that Pink isn't a good singer.

A8 ○ Music words

a) What are the music words? Write down the missing letters.

B _ _ D   G _ _   _ T _ R   _ L B _ _

wordbank
art

C _ _ _ _ S   G _ _ T _ _   R _ _ D _ _

_ O _ C _ _ T   _ U S _ _ _ _ N

_ _ _ G L _   I _ _ _ _ _ M _ _ _

_ _ E A _ _ R   R _ H _ _ _ S _ L

CD
2/22

b) Listen to the CD and check your words.

portfolio
I can work with words

c) Use the words to start a word web about music. Then add more words.

A9 ● Sound check

a) This is a song Sabrina and the Gatecrashers often sing for their fans. Complete it.

portfolio
I can learn English

Your [feɪs] ______________ we've never [siːn] ______________

To your [haʊs] ______________ we've never [biːn] ______________

But we [nəʊ] ______________ you're out [ðeə] ______________

And we really [laɪk] ______________ you – yeah

You're [wɪð] ______________ us all the [taɪm] ______________

You [lɑːf] ______________, you [dɑːns] ______________, you sing along

[kʌm] ______________ and join us in our brand new [sɒŋ] ______________

You send [ʌs] ______________ letters, ['preznts] ______________ and more

We've ['nevə] ______________ felt like this [bɪ'fɔː] ______________

You're the ['pɜːfɪkt] ______________ fan – that's [truː] ______________

So our ['mjuːsɪk] ______________ is [dʒʌst] ______________ for you.

CD
2/23

b) Listen to the CD and check your song.

A10 ○ Choose

1. Work with a partner. Partner A is a reporter for a TV programme and Partner B is a famous pop or film star. Make notes for an interview and practise it. Then act it out in class or make a video.
2. Why do so many people like casting shows? Write down at least three reasons. Then compare your ideas with a partner's and make a list. Present your ideas in class.
3. Bring your favourite music to class, play it and talk about it.
   - Say when, where and how often you listen to it.
   - Say why you like it. How does it make you feel? What do you find special about it?

B1 ● Children's art

You are in London with your parents. After you have read this advert, you want to go to the London International Gallery of Children's Art. Answer your parents' questions.

London International Gallery of Children's Art

The London International Gallery of Children's Art (LIGCA) wants to open visitors' eyes to the power of children's art. Our hope is to show the creativity of children and to promote international understanding.

At the LIGCA you can visit exhibitions of children's art from every corner of the world including artwork by local children. We also run a schools education programme, with exhibition tours and workshops in the gallery. Out of school hours, we offer art workshops and courses for 2- to 12-year-olds.

The Gallery is open
Fridays, Saturdays and Sundays: 10 am to 4 pm
Mondays through Sundays: workshops and birthday parties by appointment

Visiting the Gallery is free, but donations are always welcome.

Waterlow Park Centre
Dartmouth Park Hill • London N19 5JF

For information about our current exhibition please visit:
www.ligca.org/exhibitions.html

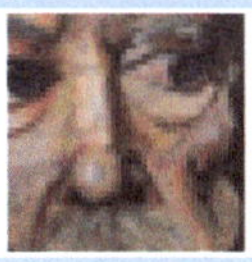

Deine Mutter: Ist das ein Museum für Bilder von Kindern aus Großbritannien?

how to ... read

Du: ______________________________

Dein Vater: Was für eine Ausstellung gibt es denn gerade?

Du: ______________________________

____

Dein Vater: Ach so. Na, dann können wir uns ja schnell in einem Internet-Café informieren. Was kostet der Eintritt?

Du: ______________________________

Deine Mutter: Na wunderbar. Hm, heute ist Donnerstag. Sieh mal nach, wie die Öffnungszeiten an Werktagen sind.

portfolio I can help out in English

Du: ______________________________

____

Dein Vater: Tja, dann lasst uns doch morgen gehen. Wo liegt das Museum?

Du: ______________________________

Deine Mutter: Hier ist unser Stadtplan. Sehen wir mal nach, wo das ist.

B2 ● Your top four places

a) Look at B1 "What's on in London?" in your textbook again. Choose your top four places or activities and write about them.

I'd like to go to the Horniman Museum because I'm interested in …
I'd like to visit … because I want …

portfolio
I can write

____

____

____

____

b) Talk to a partner and take notes on his or her answers.

What are your…?

Why would you like to go to …?

partner's name:	
his/her top four places	**reasons**

portfolio
I can talk

c) Tell the class about your partner.

… favourite places are …

He/She wants to go to … because …

B3 ○ A day in London

You are in London with your family and your best friend. Your parents allow you and your friend to spend one day on your own. They give you £20 each.

With a partner, plan the day.

how to …
work on a project, use the Internet, present

portfolio
I can talk

- Look at B1 "What's on in London?" in your textbook and Theme 6, B1 "Can you remember?" in this workbook again. Make a list of places and activities. Then look for more information on the Internet. Write down the admissions and prices for activities. You also need a one-day travelcard for £3.60 per person.
- Decide where and what you want to eat. You can use A1 "Menus" in Theme 1 in your textbook for help or you can look for places to eat on the Internet.
- Look at your list and the prices. Then decide where you want to go and what you want to do. Make notes on why you want to go there.
- Sort your new list in a good order. Where do you want to go first, second … and last? Use a map of London.
- Prepare a presentation. You can create a poster, make a transparency or use an electronic whiteboard.
- Give your talk.

B4 ● Words to describe pictures

a) When you talk about or describe a picture, you use a lot of adjectives. Make a list like this in your exercise book. Then sort the adjectives from the box into the lists.

beautiful • black • boring • cold • colourful • dangerous • interesting • scary • funny • happy • ugly • warm • depressing • white • exciting • light • tired • strange • sad • realistic

wordbank
art

Describing pictures: adjectives for …			
colours	people	atmosphere	your own opinion
bright			

Tipp
Manche Adjektive passen in mehr als eine Liste.

b) Find more adjectives and add them to your list. You can use a dictionary.

B5 ○ A classroom exhibition

a) Find a picture that you like. It can be a photocopy of a picture in a book, a postcard or a photo from a magazine.

b) What can you see in your picture? Make notes. Put up your picture in the classroom.

portfolio
I can talk

c) Have a tour through the picture gallery in your classroom. Describe your picture to your classmates. Let them guess which picture it is.

d) After the tour, choose some pictures from your class gallery. Talk about them in a group and compare them. Say why you like or don't like them.

> I like Wiebke's picture because …

> I like Doran's picture better because …

B6 Bright colours

CD 2/18

a) Listen to the CD and write these pieces of information under the right picture:

Andy Warhol, *Flowers*

Franz Marc, *Deer*[1] *in the forest II*

Gabriele Münter, *The blue lake*

Paul Klee, *Senecio (Soon an old man)*

____

____

portfolio
I can listen

____

____

b) Listen again. What is special about the pictures? Take notes.

portfolio
I can write

c) Which is your favourite picture? Describe it and say why you like it. Write the text in your exercise book.

Describe each picture in three or four sentences. Write the texts in your exercise book.

[1] deer – *Reh, Hirsch*

B7 Famous works of art

a) You can find all these works of art[1] in Theme 7 in your textbook. Choose your favourite one and tick it.

1 Louise Bourgeois
Maman (1999)

2 L.S. Lowry
Coming out of School
(1927)

3 Marc Chagall
The Blue Circus
(1950)

4 Sean Henry
Catafalque (2004)

5 Pablo Picasso
Goat (1946)

6 René Magritte
Empire of Light
(1953/54)

b) Listen to the audioguide for your work of art. Take notes in the grid.

CD 2/24 2/25 2/26 2/27 2/28 2/29

Title	
Name of artist	
Information about artist	
Information about the work of art	

how to … listen

c) Work in a group of pupils who have listened to the same audioguide. Compare your grids.

d) Get together in a group of pupils who have each listened to a different audioguide. Inform each other about your pictures.

e) With your second group, give a talk about different works of art. Everyone has to present one work of art.

[1] work of art – *Kunstwerk*

D1 Where can you find these people, animals and things? Look through Theme 7 in your textbook.

There is a bottle of water on page ____________.

There is a woman in a pink dress ____________.

There is a Chinese text on page ____________.

There is a fish with flowers on page ____________.

There are bookshelves on page ____________.

There is a girl with white earrings and a white necklace on page ____________.

D2 Put these words together. Find as many combinations as possible.

listen
work
present
look
finish
sing
make
talk
write
read

at the pictures
the information
a text
a list
to music
about music
in a group
your homework
an article
a report
to the class
to the CD
verses
to a partner

D3 Find the answers in your textbook.

1. Where can you see the UK's biggest collection of toys? ____________
2. What kind of tattoo has Pink got on her hand? ____________
3. Where does Ha Tien live? ____________
4. Where do adults pay £10 admission and under 16s are free? ____________
5. When is Tate Britain closed? ____________
6. Where is Doylestown? ____________
7. What can you find on Forest Hill? ____________

D4 Unscramble the art words.

cupiert ____________
tirnape ____________
locuro ____________
usumme ____________
tirsat ____________
hixobineit ____________

A1 ● Plans for the summer

a) Listen to Susan and Charlie. What are their plans for the summer holidays? What are they saying about Gillian's plans? Take notes.

CD 2/20

Charlie: ______________________________

____

Susan: ______________________________

____

Gillian: ______________________________

____

b) Now write about the friends' plans.

Charlie is going to ______________________________

He is going to ______________________________

Susan is going to ______________________________

She is also ______________________________

Gillian ______________________________

She ______________________________

c) Write about the holiday plans of five people you know.

____

____

____

____

____

Whose holiday plans do you like best? Say why.

A2 ● Holiday activities

**a) Match the verbs with the nouns.
Write the lists in your exercise book.**

go • visit • take • write • ask • buy • stay • have

castle • museum • picnic • hotel • way • postcards • bus • relatives • train • beach party • some sights • e-mails • souvenirs • photos • stamps • tourist information

b) Write more phrases for holiday activities with verbs from the box. Add them to the lists.

wordbank
travelling

portfolio
I can work with words

Tipp
Manchmal musst du eine Präposition oder auch einen Artikel benutzen.

A3 ● What would they do?

a) Complete the sentences with the phrases from the box.

visit his family in India more often • travel around the world with her daughter • train with a famous football star • fly to Canada in the summer holidays • see kangaroos • spend a week in New York • go to Barbados on holiday

LiF 21

portfolio I can work with words

1. If Charlie could go to the USA, *he would spend* __________
2. If Gillian had a pen friend in Toronto, *she would* __________
3. If Susan went to Australia, __________
4. If Mr Patel had more time, __________
5. If Vanessa could make a wish, __________
6. If the Batsons had enough money, __________
7. If Mrs Collins won the lottery, __________

CD 2/36

b) Listen to the CD and check your sentences.

Imagine you could travel to these places. What would you do there?

Paris | Scotland | Disneyland | the USA | China | a lonely island

If I went to Paris, I would visit __________

If I travelled to Scotland, __________

A4 ○ What if …?

Write a "what if" poem.

Model

What if __________?
I could __________.
What if __________?
I would __________.
What if __________?
I would __________.

What if summer lasted half a year?
I could go swimming for 182 days.
What if sweets were good for your teeth?
I would be my dentist's favourite patient.
What if chewing gum made you smarter?
I would be a genius, that's for sure.

A5 ● Buying a train ticket

a) Listen to the dialogue at the train station. What kind of ticket does the boy buy?

☐ a single ticket ☐ a return ticket

CD 2/23

b) What are the German words for "single ticket" and "return ticket"? Try to guess.

c) Listen to the CD again and tick the phrases you can hear.

portfolio I can listen

- ☐ How can I get to Manchester, please?
- ☐ A ticket to Manchester, please.
- ☐ OK, that's £72.50, please.
- ☐ OK, that's £27.50, please.
- ☐ I'd like to book a seat.
- ☐ Where is the platform?
- ☐ And for your information …
- ☐ All trains leave from platform three.
- ☐ All trains to Manchester leave from platform three today.
- ☐ Is the train on time?
- ☐ When is the next train, please?
- ☐ Could you tell me when the next train leaves?
- ☐ In two minutes so you'll have to hurry.
- ☐ But don't worry if you miss it.
- ☐ There's a train to Manchester every thirty minutes.

d) With a partner, act out the dialogue. e) Add the new phrases to your phrase book.

portfolio I can work with words

A6 ● Trendy trainers

a) Vicky and Jodie go shopping. Unscramble the dialogue and write it in your exercise book.

Jodie: Well, how do you feel?

Vicky: You're right, £14.99 is a good price. OK, I'll take them.

Vicky: Yes, please. I'd like to try on these trainers.

Shop assistant: Thank you. And here's your change. Have a good day. Bye.

Vicky: 5, please.

Shop assistant: Hello, can I help you?

Vicky: They fit, but I'm not sure …

portfolio I can read

Shop assistant: OK, so if you'd just follow me to the cash desk, please. So that's £14.99, please.

Vicky and **Jodie:** Bye.

Jodie: I think they look great. And they're on sale, too.

Shop assistant: Wait a moment, I'll just check. Here you are.

Vicky: Here you are.

Vicky: Thanks.

Shop assistant: Certainly. What size do you need?

b) Listen to the CD and check your dialogue.

CD 2/37

c) Work with a partner. Partner A wants to buy a pair of jeans in a clothes shop. Partner B is the shop assistant. Make up a dialogue. Then act it out in class.

portfolio I can talk

A7 ● At the youth hostel

You meet someone at a British youth hostel. Work with a partner and act out the scene.

Partner A: Reisende/Reisender

1 Stelle dich vor und frage, wie B heißt.
3 Sage, woher du kommst, und frage, woher B kommt.
5 Verneine. Sage, dass du mit deinem Vater dort bist, und frage, ob B allein reist.
7 Sage, dass du vier Tage bleibst, und frage, wie lange B bleibt.
9 Sage, das sei schade.
11 Verabschiede dich ebenfalls bis später.

Partner B: Reisende/Reisender

2 Sage, dass du Debbie/Mike heißt. Frage, woher A kommt.
4 Sage, dass du aus New York kommst. Frage dann, ob A allein reist.
6 Sage, dass du mit deiner Schwester dort bist. Frage, wie lange A bleibt.
8 Sage, dass du nur zwei Tage bleibst.
10 Sage, dass es nett war, A zu treffen, und verabschiede dich bis später.

portfolio
I can talk

You meet someone at a British youth hostel. Work with a partner and act out the scene.

Partner A: Reisende/Reisender

1 Stelle dich vor und frage, wie B heißt.
3 Sage, woher du kommst, und frage, woher B kommt.
5 Verneine. Sage, dass du mit deiner Tante dort bist, und frage, ob B allein reist.
7 Sage, dass du gestern angekommen bist.
9 Sage, dass du vier Tage bleibst, und frage, wie lange B bleibt.
11 Frage, was B vorhat.
13 Sage, dass es nett war, A zu treffen, und verabschiede dich bis später.

Partner B: Reisende/Reisender

2 Sage, dass du Britney/Ron heißt. Frage, woher A kommt.
4 Sage, dass du aus Sydney kommst. Frage dann, ob A allein reist.
6 Sage, dass du mit deinem Bruder dort bist. Frage, wann A angekommen ist.
8 Frage, wie lange A bleibt.
10 Sage, dass du nur zwei Tage bleibst.
12 Sage, dass du wandern und ein Dinosauriermuseum besichtigen möchtest.
14 Verabschiede dich ebenfalls bis später.

A8 ○ DO IT 4 Real

Look at the web page in A6 "Summer camps" in your textbook again. Then answer the questions.

1. The address of the website is www.doit4real.co.uk. What does "uk" stand for?

____

2. How many camps has DO IT 4 Real got? ______________________________

3. How long can people stay at one of the camps? ______________________________

4. For what age group are the DO IT 4 Real summer camps? ______________________________

____

5. What do you have to do if you want to come with friends? ______________________________

____

A9 Talking about camps

a) Listen to A7 "Choosing a camp" in your textbook again. What do David and Rajiv say about the different summer camps? Take notes in the grid.

CD 2/24

Camp	What Rajiv says about it	What David says about it
Musical Star Club		
Water Sports Plus		
Climbing Club		
Urban Survival		
Football and Rugby Camp		

LiF 19

b) Compare your notes with a partner's.

Rajiv says that the Football and Rugby Camp … But he also says that …

David thinks that …

A10 Sound check

a) Listen to the words on CD. Is the stress on the first, second or third syllable? Sort the words into the list.

CD 2/39

holidays	exciting	adventure	travelling	information
fantastic	situation	sightseeing	Australia	envelope
entertainment	musical	direction	application	competition

Ooo					
oOo					
ooOo					

b) Listen again and check your list.

CD 2/40

A11 Choose

1. Work in a group. Make a survey of all your classmates' plans for the holidays. Then present it in class.
2. Work in groups of three. One of you is a teenager who is going to spend his or her first holiday at a camp. The other two are the parents. What do they ask their child? What advice do they give him or her? Make up a dialogue and act it out in class.
3. Work with a partner. Use the Internet to find information about another summer camp in the UK. Make notes and print out some pictures. Then present the information in class.
4. What was your best holiday? When was it? Where did you spend the holiday? What did you do? Make notes and then give a talk.

wordbank travelling

portfolio I can talk, I can work with words

B1 ● What have they been doing?

Write down what the people have been doing and for how long.

pack suitcases • swim • write packing list • plan a weekend trip to Scotland • practise for next football match • ~~read about camps~~

LiF 22, 23

David has been reading about camps for an hour.

portfolio
I can work with grammar

B2 ● How long?

a) Answer these questions.

LiF 22, 23

1. How long have you been living in your town? For ______
2. How long have you had your schoolbag? ______
3. How long have you been going to your present school? ______
4. How long have you known your oldest friend? ______
5. How long have you had your present hairstyle? ______
6. How long have you been using computers? ______
7. How long have you been using mobile phones? ______
8. How long has your favourite teacher been teaching at your school? ______

b) Now ask your partner the questions from a). Take notes on his or her answers.

c) Report some facts about yourself and your partner to the class.

Pedram has been living in this town for eleven years.

Annika has known her oldest friend for eight years.

I have been …

B3 Where do they speak English?

a) What language do people speak in these cities? Write the names of the cities in the table. For the cities where the people don't speak English, write down the language they speak. Find help on the Internet.

~~Shanghai~~ • Nashville • Toronto • Harare • Cairo • Lublin • Port of Spain • Wellington • Colombo • Los Angeles • Islamabad • Sydney • Oslo • Buenos Aires • Sao Paulo • Cape Town • Thimphu • St Petersburg • Lilongwe

Tipp
Schau dir noch einmal das P&P und die Weltkarte im Textbook an.

English as a first language	English as a second language	city/language
		Shanghai/Chinese

b) With a partner, make a list of ten cities in different countries around the world. Then give your list to another pair. They have to say which languages are spoken there.

c) How many pupils in your class speak German as a first language? How many pupils speak German as a second language? What are these pupils' first languages? Work in a group. Make a survey and present it in class.

Work in a group. In what situations is English spoken today? When is it necessary to be able to speak English? Make a list and give examples. Present your ideas in class.

B4 If it kills me

a) Listen to the rap.

b) Listen again and underline the stressed syllables.

c) Speak the rap. Say the stressed syllables very loudly! You should sound as if you really mean what you are saying.

Create your own version of the rap. You can record it or make a video clip.

CD 2/27 2/42

I'm gonna[1] speak English if it kills me.
I'm gonna speak English if it kills me.
I'll practise day and night.
Till I know I've got it right.
I'm gonna speak English if it kills me.

I'm gonna speak English if it kills me.
I'm gonna speak English if it kills me.
I'll exercise my jaw[2]
Till it drops off on the floor.
I'm gonna speak English if it kills me.

I'm gonna speak English if it kills me.
I'm gonna speak English if it kills me.
I'll talk and talk and keep
Talking even in my sleep.
I'm gonna speak English if it kills me.

[1] gonna = going to; [2] jaw – *Kiefer*

B5 Choose

portfolio
I can write

how to ...
talk

1. Imagine you can travel around the world. Where would you go? Look at the map at the back of your textbook. Describe your route and say what you would do in the different countries.
2. In what situations have you or your family used English? Make notes. Then give a short talk in which you describe the situations.
3. Work in a group. What is fun about learning English? What is difficult? Make a list. Then present your ideas in class.

B6 Not on board

You can do some things while you are waiting at the airport which you are not allowed to do when you are on board a plane. Look at these pictures. What are you allowed to do at the airport, but not on board? Write down the rules.

you can • you may • you are allowed to

you are not allowed to • you must not

You can use your mobile phone at the airport, but you are not allowed to use it on board.

You may ______

B7 Announcements

Listen to the airport announcements and tick the right answer.

CD 2/30

1. The flight from New York is ☐ three hours late. ☐ two hours late. ☐ eight hours late.
2. Passengers to Edinburgh have to go to ☐ gate 321. ☐ gate 8. ☐ gate 78.
3. Gate number 9 will be closed ☐ in five minutes. ☐ in three minutes. ☐ in four minutes.
4. The flight from Istanbul will arrive ☐ at 10:30. ☐ at 10:40. ☐ at 10:07.
5. The flight number of the flight from Rome is ☐ 9014. ☐ 9404. ☐ 9044.
6. The gate has been changed for the flight ☐ to Paris. ☐ to Istanbul. ☐ to Berlin.

how to … listen

B8 Departures

a) Look at this departures board from Bristol Airport and find the answers.

1. When is the flight to Amsterdam? ______
2. What is the gate for the flight to Jersey? ______
3. Which airline flies to Paris? ______
4. What is the number of the flight to Brussels? ______
5. Which flights are boarding now? ______
6. Where do the passengers go who are taking the flight at 13:50? ______
7. When can the passengers to Geneva start boarding? ______
8. When can you get on the plane if you want to go to Madrid? ______
9. Monsieur Dubois from Bordeaux has just arrived at the gate. What do they tell him there?

______

b) Work with a partner. Ask each other more questions.

c) Bring a timetable (bus, underground or train) from your town or village. Work in a group. Ask each other questions.

B9 Airport talk

a) Who is saying what? Write the correct numbers in the speech bubbles.

1 Vanessa! Uncle Dan! It's great to see you!

2 Yes, I've just arrived at Heathrow.

3 All passengers for British Airways flight BA 145, please go to gate 43.

4 That's terminal 2, sir.

5 I come from New York.

6 Bye! Call me every day!

7 Excuse me. Which is the terminal for the Lufthansa flight to Berlin, please?

8 Look, it's going to land!

9 You can hand in your suitcases at the check-in counter.

10 I'll get a trolley[1].

11 I will!

12 Hi, Cheryl! Welcome to London.

b) What are some of the other people saying? Think of:

- the boy who is saying goodbye to his mother
- the two Japanese tourists
- the little boy with the Batman T-shirt
- the woman with the red hat

[1] trolley – *Gepäckwagen*

D1 You want to go to a canoeing summer camp. Pack your rucksack.

D2 Find titles for these word groups.

China – USA – Canada – Norway: ____________________

departures – arrivals – terminal – gate: ____________________

water sports – climbing – football and rugby – musical star: ____________________

June – July – August – sun: ____________________

sightseeing – beach – foreign food – no school: ____________________

D3 Look at Theme 8 and the map at the back of your textbook. Find the answers.

1. Find six activities that you can do at a summer camp.

____

2. Write down the names of six countries in which English is the official language.

____

3. Write down the names of six cities in different countries that **you** would like to visit.

____

4. How long is the flight from Heathrow Airport to Mumbai in India? ____________________
5. Where is Bala? ____________________
6. What can you see if you go to Cairo? ____________________

D4 A joke.

What did the pig say at the beach on a hot summer's day?

„I'm bacon!"

LiF 1 Mengenangaben ● much / many / a lot of

much, **many** und **a lot of** – alle drei Wörter bedeuten *viel* beziehungsweise *viele* auf Deutsch. Was ist der Unterschied?

- **many** bezeichnet eine große *Anzahl* von etwas. Es steht vor zählbaren Nomen (*count nouns*):

  Many pizzas have a lot of cheese on them.

- **much** bezeichnet eine große *Menge* von etwas. Es steht vor nicht zählbaren Nomen (*uncount nouns*):

  Well, some pizzas don't have much cheese on them.

- **many** und **much** werden vor allem in Fragen und negativen Sätzen verwendet. Sonst kannst du für *viel(e)* auch immer **a lot of** oder auch **lots of** nehmen. Dabei brauchst du nicht zwischen zählbaren und nicht zählbaren Nomen zu unterscheiden:

  I've had a lot of salad this week.
  A lot of restaurants do takeaway food.

  When she came here from India, she brought lots of spices with her.

Tipp Zählbare Nomen erkennst du leicht daran, dass sie fast immer das Mehrzahl-s tragen – aber Vorsicht: Es gibt Ausnahmen wie *children, men, women, mice* usw.! Am besten machst du dir mit anderen aus der Klasse einige Merk-Poster mit „much-words" und „many-words" darauf. Mit den Wörtern aus A6 und dem gesamten Theme 1 könnt ihr gleich anfangen.

LiF 2 Remember? Das Perfekt ● present perfect

present perfect

- drückt aus, dass eine Handlung, die in der Vergangenheit begann, in der Gegenwart noch andauert oder nachwirkt
- wird auch verwendet, wenn man sagen will, was jemand irgendwann schon einmal, schon häufig oder noch nie getan hat

• Signalwörter:	ever, never, yet, already, just, so far
• FORMEL:	*have / has + Partizip Perfekt*
(+)	She **has tried** a lot of interesting food.
(–)	She **hasn't tried** a lot of interesting food.
(Y/N) ?	**Has** she **tried** a lot of interesting food?
(WH-) ?	What **has** she **tried**?
• Partizip Perfekt	(past participle)
regelmäßig:	Infinitiv + **-ed:** cook, cooked, **cooked**; try, tried, **tried**
unregelmäßig:	verschiedene Formen, z. B. eat, ate, **eaten**

Tipp Die drei Formen (*infinitive, past form, past participle*) der unregelmäßigen Verben kannst du dir besser merken, wenn du ähnliche Formen zusammen lernst, z. B. in Reimform:

bring, brought, brought
buy, bought, bought
…

LiF 3 Einfache Vergangenheit oder Perfekt? ● simple past or present perfect?

- Mit dem *present perfect* deckt man im Englischen einen Zeitraum ab, der in der Vergangenheit angefangen hat, aber noch in die Gegenwart reicht:

  Have you ever been to an Italian restaurant? **Yes, I have.**
  (Der Zeitraum reicht von irgendwann damals bis heute.)

- Das *simple past* benutzt man bei Ereignissen und Handlungen, die vergangen und abgeschlossen sind (siehe auch LiF 11).

  What was it like? **It was good. I tried three different pizzas.**
  (Das Ereignis begann und endete in der Vergangenheit.)

⚠ Im Deutschen können wir das Präteritum *oder* das Perfekt für ein Ereignis in der Vergangenheit verwenden. Im Englischen *musst* du für Handlungen, die klar in der Vergangenheit stattfanden, das *simple past* benutzen:

Ich habe drei verschiedene Pizzen probiert.	~~I've tried three different pizzas.~~
oder:	nur:
Ich probierte drei verschiedene Pizzen.	**I tried three different pizzas.**

LiF 4 Bestätigungsfragen ● question tags

- Eine Bestätigungsfrage gibt das Signal: Ich möchte, dass du mir zustimmst – wir sind doch einer Meinung, oder? Dazu benutzt man im Englischen Anhängsel wie … **can't you?** oder … **isn't it?**:

  You can read Chinese, can't you?

  He is a good cook, isn't he?

  Auf Deutsch sagen wir normalerweise *nicht wahr?* oder wir benutzen, je nach Gegend, Dialektformen wie zum Beispiel *gell?, woll?, wa?*

- So leicht wie im Deutschen ist das mit den englischen Bestätigungsfragen aber nicht. Du musst die <u>Verbform</u> immer noch einmal wiederholen und dabei n't anhängen, die Kurzform von **not**.

  You <u>are</u> chewing gum, aren't you?
  Curry <u>can</u> be very hot, can't it?
  Rajiv <u>has</u> got extra-hot chilli paste, hasn't he?

- Wenn ein Hauptverb allein steht, also nicht von einem Hilfsverb oder Modalverb begleitet wird, musst du für das Anhängsel **do** oder **does** bzw. **did** nehmen:

  You really <u>like</u> spaghetti, don't you?
  Rajiv <u>loves</u> cooking, doesn't he?
  Vanessa <u>helped</u> with the cooking, didn't she?

- Noch eine Schwierigkeit, die wir aus dem Deutschen nicht kennen: <u>Eigennamen</u> und <u>Nomen</u> musst du in der Bestätigungsfrage immer durch das passende Pronomen ersetzen:

  she
  <u>Vanessa</u> likes banana raita, doesn't ~~Vanessa~~?

  they
  <u>Rosemary and Rajiv</u> think the food is delicious, don't ~~Rosemary and Rajiv~~?

  they
  <u>Indian curries</u> are hot, aren't ~~Indian curries~~?

LiF 5 Die ing-Form als Nomen ● ing-nouns

- Wenn du im Deutschen ein Verb zu einem Nomen umformen willst, brauchst du einfach nur den Infinitiv großzuschreiben. Im Englischen benutzt man dafür die ing-Form des Verbs:

  walking (das) Gehen **jumping** (das) Springen

- Die ing-Form als Nomen kann im Satz dieselben Aufgaben übernehmen wie jedes andere Nomen. Sie kann als Subjekt stehen:

  Stepping on and off a chair ten times was no problem.
  Doing press-ups was difficult.
  Walking in the forest can be dangerous.

  Oder als Objekt:

  I love watching football.
  I like playing hockey.

- Bei einigen ing-Formen musst du besonders auf die Schreibweise achten: Endet der Infinitiv des Verbs auf **-e**, dann fällt das **-e** in der ing-Form weg. Bei einigen Infinitiven wird der letzte Buchstabe verdoppelt.

make	making
take	taking
dance	dancing
sit	sitting
run	running
hop	hopping

LiF 6 Remember? Vergleichsformen des Adjektivs ● comparison

Vergleichsformen des Adjektivs

Hier kannst du sehen, welche Vergleichsform du wann anwenden musst:

• einsilbige Adjektive:	tall, tall**er**, tall**est**
• zweisilbige Adjektive, wenn sie auf **-y**, **-le**, **-er**, **-ow** enden:	clever, clever**er**, clever**est**
• Adjektive mit zwei oder mehr Silben:	successful, **more** successful, **most** successful
• Hier wird der Konsonant verdoppelt:	big, bigg**er**, bigg**est**

LiF 7 be able to

- **be able to** drückt die Fähigkeit aus, etwas zu tun; es bedeutet also dasselbe wie **can**.

  The boy is able to play football.
  The man with the black hair is not able to smell anything.

- Im *simple past* benutzt du **was able to** oder **were able to**. Allerdings kannst du auch **could** verwenden:

  Christy's brothers made him a box on wheels, so he was able to play with them.
  They built a little house in the garden for him where he could write his stories, read and draw.

- Da **can** nicht in allen Zeitformen stehen kann *musst* du manchmal **be able to** verwenden, so z. B. auch im *will-future*:

  The boy will be able to play football again next week.
  The old lady won't be able to eat very much.

Du wirst dieses Fahrrad nicht reparieren können.

Tipp

Malt euch ein Merk-Poster zu **can** / **be able to**. So könnte es aussehen:

infinitive	simple past	present perfect	simple present	will-future
can	could	–	can	–
be able to	was able to were able to	have been able to has been able to	am able to are able to is able to	will be able to

LiF 8 Relativsätze ● relative clauses

- Wenn du eine Sache oder eine Person näher beschreiben willst, kannst du einen Relativsatz verwenden:

  There are a lot of dancers and brightly coloured floats that pass by in the parade
  – and the tourists who take photos**.**
  The police put up posters which tell everybody to be careful**.**

- Englische Relativsätze fangen meistens mit **who**, **which** oder **that** an. **who** kannst du nur für Personen nehmen, **which** geht nur für Dinge. **that** kannst du für Personen und für Dinge verwenden:

There are police officers	who that	**help people.**
There is a programme	which that	**tells you what's on.**

Tipp Mit diesem Spiel könnt ihr die Verwendung von **who** und **which** in Relativsätzen üben: Legt in eurem Klassenraum eine „**who**-Seite" und eine „**which**-Seite" fest. Eine Spielleiterin oder ein Spielleiter eurer Wahl ruft euch dann Nomen zu und ihr müsst schnell auf die richtige Seite laufen.

Beispiel:	"**dancer**"	→	**who**-Seite
	"**band**"	→	**which**-Seite
	usw.		

LiF 9 Remember? Die Verlaufsform der Gegenwart ● present progressive

present progressive

- gibt an, was gerade eben geschieht
- FORMEL:

FORMEL:	(BE) + (VERB)+**ing**
(+)	He **is watching** the parade.
(–)	He **isn't watching** the parade.
(Y/N) ?	**Is** he **watching** the parade?
(WH-) ?	What **is** he **watching**?

LiF 10 Die Verlaufsform der Vergangenheit ● past progressive

- Das *past progressive* drückt aus, dass eine Handlung in der Vergangenheit über einen längeren Zeitraum im Gange war.
  The boy was watching **the parade.**

- Wenn zwei Ereignisse in der Vergangenheit gleichzeitig ablaufen, dann bildet das länger andauernde den „Hintergrund" für das kürzere, das sich im „Vordergrund" abspielt. Wir können im Deutschen zum Beispiel sagen: „Ich war gerade am Kochen, als der Briefträger klingelte." Das, was man im Deutschen mit „ich war gerade am Kochen" oder „ich war gerade dabei, zu kochen" ausdrücken kann, das sagt man im Englischen mit dem *past progressive.*
  Vordergrund-Geschehen: **John Scott had a narrow escape yesterday**
  Hintergrund-Geschehen: **while he** was watching **the carnival parade.**

- Die Formen des *past progressive* werden genauso gebildet wie die Formen des *present progressive.* Nur steht **be** natürlich in der entsprechenden Vergangenheitsform:

FORMEL	**was / were** + (VERB)+**ing**
(+)	**You were stealing wallets.**
(–)	**I wasn't stealing wallets.**
(Y/N)?	**Were you watching TV?**
(WH-)?	**What were you watching?**

LiF 11 Remember? Die einfache Vergangenheit ● simple past

simple past

• steht für Ereignisse in der Vergangenheit	
• Signalwörter:	yesterday, last night, last week, last month, last year, a week ago, a month ago, a year ago, …
• FORMEL:	(VERB) + **ed** / *past form*
(+)	I miss**ed** my home and my family.
(–)	I **didn't miss** my teachers.
(Y/N) ?	**Did** you **miss** your family? – **Did** you **eat** spiders?
(WH-) ?	Who **did** you **miss** most? – What **did** you **eat**?
• unregelmäßige Verben:	eat ist ein Beispiel für ein unregelmäßiges Verb. Hier gilt die Grundregel *Infinitiv* + **ed** nicht; du musst diese Formen auswendig lernen. Lies auch den Tipp unten auf S. 96.
• **be**	hat besondere Vergangenheitsformen: I **was** / he **was** / she **was** / it **was** you **were** / we **were** / they **were**

LiF 12 Die Stellung der Satzglieder ● word order

- In jeder Sprache haben die Sätze einen Bauplan. Der Bauplan englischer Sätze ist ziemlich strikt – aber auch ziemlich klar. Hier ist das Grundmuster für einfache Sätze:

0 (VORFELD)	1 SUBJEKT	2 PRÄDIKAT	3 OBJEKT
	I	**missed**	**my home.**
No,	**I**	**didn't brush**	**my teeth.**
Yes,	**I**	**was afraid.**	
Well,	**I**	**would go back**	**for a holiday.**

- Dieser Bauplan bleibt auch in Fragesätzen bestehen. Das ist im Deutschen nicht so. (Deshalb kommen wir manchmal in Schwierigkeiten und verdrehen die Satzglieder.)

0 FRAGESIGNAL	1 SUBJEKT	2 PRÄDIKAT	3 OBJEKT
What did	**you**	**miss?**	
Did	**you**	**brush**	**your teeth?**
Were	**you**	**afraid?**	
Would	**you**	**go back?**	

- Zeitangaben und Ortsangaben stehen immer außerhalb des Kernsatzes. Wenn sie zusammen in einem Satz vorkommen, steht immer „Ort" vor „Zeit":

KERNSATZ (SUBJEKT-PRÄDIKAT-OBJEKT)	ORTSANGABE	ZEITANGABE
Robinson lived	**on the island**	**for many years.**
He and Friday arrived	**in York**	**on 11th June 1687.**

Tipp Wenn dir Merksätze helfen, probier's mit diesem: Like nine before ten, it's "where" before "when".

Eine Zeitangabe kann aber auch *vor* dem Kernsatz stehen:

ZEITANGABE	KERNSATZ (SUBJEKT-PRÄDIKAT-OBJEKT)	ORTSANGABE
On 11th June 1687	**he and Friday arrived**	**in York.**

LiF 13 Der Infinitiv mit to ● to-infinitive

- Nach Verbformen wie **would like**, **would love**, **would hate** musst du immer einen Infinitiv mit **to** verwenden:

  He would like to talk to girls in class.
  Die Kurzform von **would** lautet **'d**. **He'd like to talk to girls in class.**

- Vorsicht! Auch nach **want** steht der Infinitiv mit **to**: **She wants to run away from home.**

LiF 14 have to

- **have to** benutzt man, um eine Notwendigkeit auszudrücken:

  We have to use electricity for cooking.
  When we had no electricity, we had to use candles.

- In den meisten Zeitformen musst du **have to** anstelle von **must** verwenden:

INFINITIVE	SIMPLE PAST	PRESENT PERFECT	SIMPLE PRESENT	WILL-FUTURE
must	–	–	**must**	–
have to	**had to**	**have had to** **has had to**	**have to** **has to**	**will have to**

LiF 15 Das Passiv ● the passive

- Wenn der Urheber einer Handlung nicht von Bedeutung ist, verwendet man oft das Passiv:

  The Amphicar was invented in 1961.

- Verbformen im Passiv bildest du mit **be** und dem Partizip des Hauptverbs. Die Grundform im Passiv lautet bei **invent** zum Beispiel: **be invented** – erfunden werden. Jetzt musst du nur noch **be** in die jeweils passende Zeitform setzen – und fertig:

	(BE)	PARTIZIP	
Matches	**are**	**used**	**to make fire.**
Pedal power	**was**	**used**	**to pump water into the shower.**

- Wenn du in einem Passiv-Satz doch einmal den Urheber nennen willst, musst du ihn mit **by** angeben:

  The Amphicar was designed by Hans Trippel. **The first machines were powered by water.**

LiF 16 Bedingungssätze 1 ● conditional clauses 1

- Wenn du sagen willst, was unter bestimmten Bedingungen geschehen wird oder geschehen kann, benutzt du einen Bedingungssatz:

  If I sell my old toys, I can earn some extra money.
  If you are short of money, you can do the shopping for someone.
  If they sell enough, they'll have some extra money for the trip.

- Im if-Satz (*if-clause*) benutzt du ein Verb im *simple present*. Im Hauptsatz (*main clause*) muss ein Modalverb (hier **will**, **can** oder **must**) mit einem Hauptverb stehen:

IF-CLAUSE	MAIN CLAUSE
If I do a paper round,	**I will earn some extra money.**
If I do a paper round,	**I can earn some extra money.**
If you are in a wheelchair,	**you must start at 9.25 from the Green Start.**

Tipp Die meisten Bedingungssätze fangen mit **if** an, deshalb werden sie auch „if-Sätze" genannt. Du darfst hier niemals **when** statt **if** benutzen, obwohl es vom Deutschen her so vertraut klingt. Wenn du einen deutschen Satz mit „wenn" hast, probiere aus, ob du auch „falls" sagen könntest – wenn das geht, benutzt du im Englischen **if**; wenn das nicht geht, benutzt du **when**.

LiF 17 something / anything

- **something** und **anything** bedeuten beide „etwas" auf Deutsch. In normalen Aussagesätzen verwendest du **something**:

  Now that's something very special.

- In Fragesätzen nimmst du im Allgemeinen **anything**:

  Have you got anything really old?

- Wenn du etwas anbietest oder um etwas bittest, ist es allerdings besser, **something** zu verwenden, denn damit zeigst du, dass du ein „ja" erwartest:

  Would you like to give something for our car boot sale?

- In negativen Sätzen nimmst du **anything**:

  I didn't find anything interesting.

  I've never seen anything like that before.

LiF 18 Remember? some / (not) any

some / (not) any

• im einfachen Satz:	I need **some milk** for my cornflakes.
	There are **some apples** on the cupboard.
• bei einer Frage:	– Normalfall:
	Have we got **any milk**?
	Are there **any cornflakes** in the cupboard?
	– „ja" wird erwartet:
	Can I have **some milk**, please?
• in Verbindung mit **not**:	No, we have**n't** got **any** cornflakes left.
	There's **never any** milk in this house.

LiF 19 Berichtete Rede 1 ● reported speech 1

- Wenn du berichten willst, was jemand gesagt hat, benutzt du die Form der berichteten (indirekten) Rede:

	BEGLEITSATZ *(report clause)*	WIEDERGEGEBENE AUSSAGE *(reported clause)*
"We could do with a break."	**Sabrina says that**	**they could do with a break.**

- Berichtete Rede besteht aus einem Begleitsatz und der wiedergegebenen Aussage. Beide Satzteile können, müssen aber nicht unbedingt durch **that** verbunden werden.

- Wenn die Originalaussage Wörter enthält, die nur aus dem Zusammenhang richtig zu verstehen sind, musst du sie in der wiedergegebenen Aussage anpassen:

"We**'re helping Sabrina.**"	**Susan says (that) they're helping Sabrina.**
"I**'m exhausted.**"	**Sabrina says (that) she's exhausted.**

Notting Hill Gate 3A

Portfolio-Fragebögen

Name: ______________________________

Klasse: ______________

Diesterweg®

Liebe Schülerin, lieber Schüler,

Portfolio-Fragebögen kennst du schon aus den letzten beiden Schuljahren. Ab diesem Jahr sehen die Fragebögen etwas anders aus, an der Vorgehensweise ändert sich aber nichts. Du füllst die Fragebögen jedes Mal aus, wenn ihr ein *Theme* im *Textbook* (TB) und *Workbook* (WB) komplett abgeschlossen habt.

Falls du vergessen hast, wie das geht, lies diese Anleitung:

Sieh dir z. B. die Sätze zum *Hören* an. Lies die Sätze und überlege, wie gut du das kannst, was dort beschrieben ist. Hinter jedem Satz steht, wo du nachschlagen kannst, wenn du nicht genau weißt, was gemeint ist.

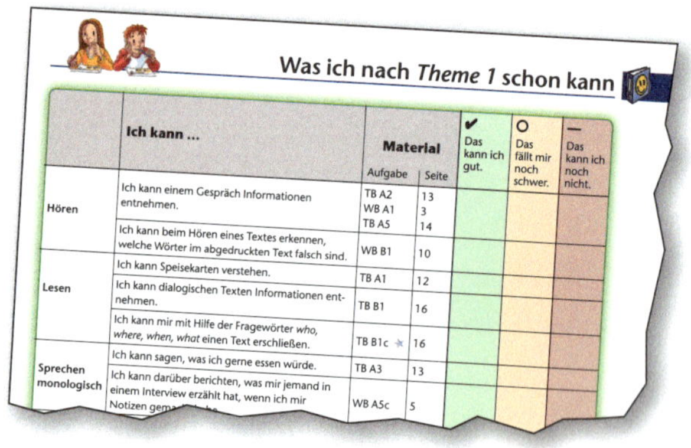

Was ich nach *Theme 1* schon kann

	Ich kann …	Material Aufgabe	Seite	✔ Das kann ich gut.	O Das fällt mir noch schwer.	— Das kann ich noch nicht.
Hören	Ich kann einem Gespräch Informationen entnehmen.	TB A2 WB A1 TB A5	13 3 14			
	Ich kann beim Hören eines Textes erkennen, welche Wörter im abgedruckten Text falsch sind.	WB B1	10			
Lesen	Ich kann Speisekarten verstehen.	TB A1	12			
	Ich kann dialogischen Texten Informationen entnehmen.	TB B1	16			
	Ich kann mir mit Hilfe der Fragewörter *who, where, when, what* einen Text erschließen.	TB B1c	16			
Sprechen monologisch	Ich kann sagen, was ich gerne essen würde.	TB A3	13			
	Ich kann darüber berichten, was mir jemand in einem Interview erzählt hat, wenn ich mir Notizen gem…	WB A5c	5			

Es kann auch sein, dass ihr im Unterricht nicht alle Übungen gemacht habt. Dann kannst du den betreffenden Satz überspringen.

Hinter jedem Satz kannst du ein Symbol eintragen, das zeigt, wie gut du etwas schon kannst.

Wenn du meinst, dass du etwas schon gut kannst, dann mache in der grünen Spalte ein Häkchen ✔.

Dir fällt etwas noch schwer? Dann male einen Kreis O in die gelbe Spalte. Lies dann die angegebene Stelle im *Textbook* (TB) oder *Workbook* (WB) nach. Hier kannst du dann noch einmal üben.

Wenn du etwas noch nicht kannst, dann mache einen Strich — in der roten Spalte. Sieh dir die passenden Stellen im TB und WB noch einmal ganz genau an. Am besten blätterst du dann zurück zu den vorigen Fragebögen und schaust nach, wie du deine Kenntnisse dort eingeschätzt hast. Du kannst dir dann noch einmal die passenden Stellen im TB und im WB anschauen.

Auf der letzten Seite findest du einen Fragebogen, in den du am Ende der Klasse 7 eintragen kannst, was dir besonders gut beim Englischlernen geholfen hat.

Und jetzt: Viel Spaß!

Was ich nach *Theme 1* schon kann

	Ich kann …	**Material** Aufgabe	Seite	✔ Das kann ich gut.	O Das fällt mir noch schwer.	— Das kann ich noch nicht.
Hören	Ich kann einem Gespräch Informationen entnehmen.	TB A2 WB A1 TB A5	13 3 14			
	Ich kann beim Hören eines Textes erkennen, welche Wörter im abgedruckten Text falsch sind.	WB B1	10			
Lesen	Ich kann Speisekarten verstehen.	TB A1	12			
	Ich kann dialogischen Texten Informationen entnehmen.	TB B1	16			
	Ich kann mir mit Hilfe der Fragewörter *who, where, when, what* einen Text erschließen.	TB B1c ★	16			
Sprechen monologisch	Ich kann sagen, was ich gerne essen würde.	TB A3	13			
	Ich kann darüber berichten, was mir jemand in einem Interview erzählt hat, wenn ich mir Notizen gemacht habe.	WB A5c	5			
Sprechen dialogisch	Ich kann eine Bestellung im Restaurant machen und auf die Fragen des Kellners antworten.	WB A1d	3			
	Ich kann fragen, was jemand schon mal gemacht hat und auf solche Fragen antworten.	TB A9c	15			
Schreiben	Ich kann eine Speisekarte auf Englisch schreiben.	TB A4 2., 3.	13			
	Ich kann einen Restaurantdialog schreiben.	TB A8 ☼ TB B5b	15 18			
	Ich kann einen Text über ein besonderes Erlebnis schreiben, das mit dem Thema Essen zu tun hat.	WB A11	9			
	Ich kann einen Text über landestypisches Essen schreiben, wenn ich eine Vorlage habe.	TB B6b	23			
Sprach-mittlung	Ich kann in einem deutschen Restaurant einem englischen Partner bei der Bestellung aushelfen.	WB A7	7			
	Ich kann auf Deutsch erklären, wie man ein Gericht zubereitet, wenn ich ein englisches Rezept habe.	WB B7	13			
Lern- und Arbeits-techniken	Ich kann in der *wordbank* nachschlagen, wenn mir Wörter bzw. Ausdrücke fehlen.	WB A11	9			
	Ich kann meine Lösungen mit Hilfe der CD überprüfen und verbessern.	WB A10 TB B3b	9 18			
Wortschatz	Ich kenne Redemittel, um zu begründen, warum ich in ein bestimmtes Restaurant gehen will.	TB A3b	13			
	Ich kenne Redemittel, um mich bei einem Restaurantbesuch zu verständigen.	TB A8 TB B5	15 18			
	Ich kann ein *word web* zum Thema Essen erstellen.	TB B4	18			
Sprachliche Mittel	Ich kann *much, many* oder *a lot of* als Mengenangaben verwenden.	TB A6 WB A4	14 5			
	Ich kann *present perfect* und *past tense* richtig anwenden, wenn ich dazu Hilfen bekomme.	TB A9 TB P6	15 25			
	Ich kann *question tags* verwenden.	TB B3 WB B3	18 11			
	Ich kann eine grammatische Regel ableiten.	TB A6 TB B3	14 18			

Was ich nach *Theme 2* schon kann

	Ich kann …	Material Aufgabe	Seite	✔ Das kann ich gut.	O Das fällt mir noch schwer.	— Das kann ich noch nicht.
Hören	Ich kann verstehen, was jemand zum Thema Sport erzählt.	TB A3 WB A6	30 18			
	Ich kann verstehen, welches Gesundheitsproblem die Personen haben.	TB B2 WB B3	35 22			
Lesen	Ich kann schriftliche Anweisungen verstehen, wenn Bilder dabei helfen.	TB A2 WB A2	29 16			
	Ich kann gezielt nach Informationen im Text suchen.	TB A3 WB A12	30 20			
	Ich kann einen längeren Text über die Lebensgeschichte einer Person verstehen.	TB B4	36			
Sprechen monologisch	Ich kann über eine Sportart sprechen, die ich regelmäßig mache oder schaue.	TB A4	31			
	Ich kann berichten, wie schwer oder leicht die Fitness-Übungen für mich waren.	TB A2c	29			
	Ich kann mit Hilfe meiner Notizen eine Person und ihre Lieblingssportart vorstellen.	TB A3c WB A5b	30 17			
Sprechen dialogisch	Ich kann mit Hilfe von Notizen mit einem Partner einen Dialog zum Thema Fitness vorspielen.	WB A1	15			
	Ich kann in einem Interview Fragen über die Lieblingssportart stellen.	TB A4 1. WB A5a	28 17			
	Ich kann mit Hilfe von Rollenkarten ein Rollenspiel zum Thema Arztbesuch vorführen.	WB B4	22			
Schreiben	Ich kann über meine Sportart schreiben.	TB A4b	31			
	Ich kann über einen Sportler schreiben.	WB A12	20			
	Ich kann eine Anweisung für eine Sportübung aufschreiben.	WB A2	16			
Sprach-mittlung	Ich kann bei einem Arztbesuch sprachlich vermitteln.	WB B2	21			
Lern- und Arbeits-techniken	Ich kann wichtige Informationen aus dem Text in einer Tabelle notieren.	TB A3b	30			
	Ich kann die Bedeutung von Wörtern im Wörterbuch nachschlagen.	TB A5 TB B1c	32 34			
Wortschatz	Ich kann Körperteile und Gesundheitsprobleme benennen.	WB B1	21			
	Ich kenne Wörter, die man braucht um Sportübungen zu beschreiben.	WB A2	16			
Sprachliche Mittel	Ich kann die ing-Form als Nomen benutzen, wenn ich über Sportarten spreche oder schreibe.	WB A6 TB P3	18 38			
	Ich kann über die Eigenschaften von Personen oder Dingen sprechen und sie vergleichen.	TB A5c	32			
	Ich kann sagen, was jemand (nicht) tun kann.	TB B3 WB B7	35 24			

Was ich nach *Theme 3* schon kann

	Ich kann ...	Material Aufgabe	Seite	✔ Das kann ich gut.	O Das fällt mir noch schwer.	— Das kann ich noch nicht.
Hören	Ich kann eine gehörte Geschichte verstehen, wenn ich schon etwas über das Thema weiß.	TB A3	43			
	Ich kann einem Interview gezielt Informationen entnehmen.	TB A7 TB B3	49 53			
	Ich kann einem Hörtext entnehmen, wer den Karneval mag und wer nicht.	WB A7a	31			
Lesen	Ich kann einer Geschichte entnehmen, wo jemand ist und was er macht.	TB A4	46			
	Ich kann kurze Blog-Einträge verstehen, wenn ich über das Thema schon etwas weiß.	TB A5	47			
	Ich kann einen kurzen Zeitungsartikel verstehen.	TB B1	51			
Sprechen monologisch	Ich kann darüber sprechen, wie Leute Karneval feiern.	TB A1 WB A1	42 27			
	Ich kann eine Präsentation über ein Straßenfest halten.	TB A10	49			
Sprechen dialogisch	Ich kann mich darüber unterhalten, was auf Bildern zu sehen ist.	TB A1a TB B1	42 51			
	Ich kann fragen, was jemand zu einem bestimmten Zeitpunkt in der Vergangenheit gerade gemacht hat, wenn ich Hilfen bekomme.	TB B4	53			
	Ich kann in einem Rollenspiel ein Interview zwischen einem Polizisten und einem Zeugen durchführen, wenn ich mir vorher Notizen gemacht habe.	WB B1	34			
Schreiben	Ich kann eine Geschichte zu Ende schreiben, wenn mir Bilder dabei helfen.	WB A5	29			
	Ich kann einen Blog-Eintrag zum Thema Notting Hill Carnival schreiben, wenn ich eine Vorlage habe.	TB A5c	47			
	Ich kann aufschreiben, was der Zeuge eines Vorfalls der Polizei berichten kann.	WB B1	34			
Sprach-mittlung	Ich kann den Inhalt eines kurzen englischen Artikels auf Deutsch wiedergeben.	TB B1d	51			
	Ich kann den Inhalt eines kurzen deutschen Artikels auf Englisch wiedergeben.	WB B2	34			
Lern- und Arbeits-techniken	Ich kann eine Tabelle mit den Fragewörtern *when, where, who, what* und *why* verwenden, um besser zu verstehen, worum es in einem Bericht geht.	TB A10	49			
	Ich kann mir Notizen machen, während ich zuhöre.	TB B5b	53			
Wortschatz	Ich kenne Wörter zum Thema Karneval.	TB A1	42			
	Ich kann die Übersetzung von vorgegebenen deutschen Satzteilen in einem englischen Text finden.	TB B1c	51			
Sprachliche Mittel	Ich kann Personen und Dinge genauer beschreiben, indem ich Relativsätze benutze, aber ich brauche dazu noch Hilfe.	TB A4b TB P2	46 54			
	Ich kann beschreiben, was jemand zu einem bestimmten Zeitpunkt in der Vergangenheit gerade gemacht hat.	TB B4 WB B6	53 36			

Was ich nach *Theme 4* schon kann

	Ich kann …	Material Aufgabe	Seite	✔ Das kann ich gut.	O Das fällt mir noch schwer.	— Das kann ich noch nicht.
Hören	Ich kann einem Gespräch Informationen entnehmen.	TB A6	62			
	Ich kann verstehen, in welcher Reihenfolge über verschiedene Themen gesprochen wird.	WB B3a	45			
	Ich kann heraushören, welche Aussagen zu einem Hörtext falsch sind, und diese korrigieren.	WB B3c	45			
Lesen	Ich kann einen einfachen Comic verstehen.	TB A1	58			
	Ich kann Briefe über persönliche Probleme von Jugendlichen verstehen.	TB B1	64			
	Ich kann einen Text über das Familienleben einer Person verstehen.	TB B3	66			
Sprechen monologisch	Ich kann einen kurzen Vortrag über eine Geschichte halten, wenn ich mir Notizen dazu gemacht habe.	WB A3	39			
	Ich kann mit Hilfe von Notizen über eine Person sprechen.	TB B3b WB B7	67 47			
	Ich kann mit Hilfe von Notizen berichten, was ich tun würde, wenn ich in ein fernes Land reisen könnte.	TB P6	69			
Sprechen dialogisch	Ich kann in einem Gespräch sagen, was ich von einer Geschichte halte, und meine Meinung begründen.	WB A2b	39			
	Ich kann in einem Gespräch Fragen stellen und antworten, wenn ich über das Thema Bescheid weiß.	TB A3	60			
	Ich kann in einem Gespräch meine Meinung äußern.	TB A4c TB B2	61 65			
Schreiben	Ich kann die Handlung einer Geschichte wiedergeben, wenn ich Hilfe bekomme.	TB A2	60			
	Ich kann eine Abenteuergeschichte planen und schreiben.	WB A8	42			
	Ich kann beschreiben, wie sich eine Person fühlt.	TB B1c	65			
	Ich kann einen Brief beantworten, in dem ein Jugendlicher ein Problem beschreibt, wenn ich dazu einen *model text* habe.	TB B2b WB B4	65 46			
Sprachmittlung	Ich kann die wichtigsten Informationen in einer deutschen Ferienbroschüre auf Englisch wiedergeben.	WB A10	43			
Lern- und Arbeitstechniken	Ich kann mir zu einem Lesetext Notizen machen.	TB B3b	67			
	Ich kann vorgegebene Notizen benutzen, um einen Brief zu schreiben.	WB B4	46			
	Ich kann ein Wörterbuch benutzen.	TB P4	68			
Wortschatz	Ich kann ein *word web* zum Thema *home* erstellen.	TB A10	63			
	Ich kenne Wörter, um positive und negative Gefühle zu beschreiben.	TB B1c WB B2	65 45			
Sprachliche Mittel	Ich kann die Verbformen in der Vergangenheit anwenden.	WB A5 TB P3	40 68			
	Ich kann vorgegebene Wörter in die richtige Reihenfolge bringen.	WB A6 TB P5	41 69			
	Ich kann den Infinitiv mit *to* verwenden.	WB B6 TB P6	47 69			

Was ich nach *Theme 5* schon kann

	Ich kann …	**Material** Aufgabe	Seite	✔ Das kann ich gut.	O Das fällt mir noch schwer.	— Das kann ich noch nicht.
Hören	Ich kann mir zu einem Gespräch gezielt Notizen machen.	TB A3 WB A9	74 54			
	Ich kann einem Hörtext über eine Erfindung gezielt Informationen entnehmen.	TB B5	79			
	Ich kann heraushören, welche Aussagen zu einem Hörtext falsch sind, und diese korrigieren.	WB B7 ★	58			
Lesen	Ich kann einem kurzen Text gezielt Informationen entnehmen.	TB A2	73			
	Ich kann aus dem Satzzusammenhang fehlende Wörter ergänzen.	WB B1	55			
	Ich kann Einzelheiten aus einem längeren Bericht verstehen.	TB B1	77			
Sprechen monologisch	Ich kann erzählen und begründen, was ich mir in einem Museum gerne anschauen würde.	TB A2c TB A4	73 74			
	Ich kann einen kurzen Vortrag über eine Erfindung halten.	WB B8 2., 3.	58			
Sprechen dialogisch	Ich kann mich darüber unterhalten, wofür man alles Strom braucht.	TB A6	76			
	Ich kann zusammen mit einem Partner einen Dialog vorführen, wenn ich mir dazu Notizen gemacht habe.	WB A10 3.	54			
Schreiben	Ich kann über Erfindungen schreiben.	WB A3 TB B2c	51 72			
	Ich kann über das Leben von Robinson Crusoe schreiben, wenn mir Bilder dabei helfen.	WB A8	53			
	Ich kann eine Geschichte schreiben, wenn mir Bilder dabei helfen.	WB A11	54			
Sprach-mittlung	Ich kann einem englischen Schüler Fragen über ein Museum beantworten, wenn ich dazu ein Informationsblatt auf Deutsch habe.	WB A5	52			
Lern- und Arbeits-techniken	Ich kann meine Lösungen mit Hilfe der CD überprüfen.	WB A6 WB B4	53 56			
	Ich kann Wörter, die ich brauche, in der *wordbank* zu *science* nachschlagen.	TB A5	74			
Wortschatz	Ich kenne Wörter, um über Erfindungen zu sprechen.	TB A5 TB B3	74 79			
	Ich kann bei Wörtern die fehlenden Vokale ergänzen, wenn ich das Themengebiet kenne.	TB P2	80			
Sprachliche Mittel	Ich kann ausdrücken, was jemand tun muss oder tun musste.	TB A6 WB A8	76 53			
	Ich kann Aussagen im Passiv verwenden, wenn ich Hilfe bekomme.	WB B3 TB P6	56 81			

Was ich nach *Theme 6* schon kann

	Ich kann …	Material Aufgabe	Seite	✔ Das kann ich gut.	O Das fällt mir noch schwer.	— Das kann ich noch nicht.
Hören	Ich kann einem Gespräch gezielt Informationen entnehmen.	TB A5 TB A7	86 87			
	Ich kann auf einem Stadtplan die beschriebene Route nachverfolgen.	TB B2b	84			
	Ich kann markieren, in welcher Reihenfolge Londoner Sehenswürdigkeiten genannt werden.	WB B3	69			
Lesen	Ich kann einem Text über einen Flohmarkt wichtige Informationen entnehmen.	WB A4	63			
	Ich kann falsche Aussagen zu dem Inhalt eines Lesetextes erkennen und korrigieren.	WB A4 WB B2	63 68			
	Ich kann einen Zeitungsartikel über den *London Marathon* verstehen.	TB B1 TB B3	89 91			
Sprechen monologisch	Ich kann berichten, was mein Partner mir zum Thema Taschengeld erzählt hat.	TB A1	84			
	Ich kann mit Hilfe von Notizen eine kurze Präsentation über eine berühmte Person halten.	WB A12	67			
	Ich kann in der Klasse meine Ideen für eine *Fundraising*-Aktivität vorstellen.	TB B6	93			
Sprechen dialogisch	Ich kann in einem Interview zum Thema Taschengeld Fragen oder Antworten formulieren.	TB A1	84			
	Ich kann ein Verkaufsgespräch führen, wenn mir Rollenkarten oder eigene Notizen dabei helfen.	TB A6c WB A8	86 65			
Schreiben	Ich kann einen Artikel über ein Thema schreiben, worüber ich schon einiges weiß.	TB B4	92			
	Ich kann eine Geschichte schreiben, wenn mir Bilder dabei helfen.	WB B8	71			
	Ich kann über meine Erfahrungen auf dem Flohmarkt schreiben.	TB P4	94			
Sprachmittlung	Ich kann den Inhalt eines englischen Artikels kurz auf Deutsch wiedergeben.	WB B4b	69			
Lern- und Arbeitstechniken	Ich kann zusammen mit einem Partner ein Verkaufsgespräch vorbereiten.	TB A6c	86			
	Ich kann mir beim Schreiben eines Textes Tipps aus den How-to-Seiten holen.	TB B4	92			
	Ich kann in einem Text wichtige Stellen unterstreichen.	WB B4	69			
Wortschatz	Ich kenne Redewendungen, die ich in einem Verkaufsgespräch benutzen kann.	TB A6	86			
	Ich kann auch kompliziertere Zahlen aus einem Text heraushören und aufschreiben.	TB P7	95			
Sprachliche Mittel	Ich kann sagen, was unter bestimmten Bedingungen passiert, wenn ich Hilfen bekomme.	WB A10 WB B6	66 70			
	Ich kann *some* und *something* sowie *any* und *anything* richtig anwenden.	WB A6 TB P6	64 95			

Was ich nach *Theme 7* schon kann

	Ich kann …	**Material** Aufgabe	Seite	✔ Das kann ich gut.	O Das fällt mir noch schwer.	— Das kann ich noch nicht.
Hören	Ich kann einen Radiobericht verstehen, wenn ich vorher weiß, um welches Thema es geht.	TB A4 WB A3	99 75			
	Ich kann mit Hilfe eines Hörtextes Kunstwerke und Namen zuordnen.	WB B6	82			
Lesen	Ich kann einem Magazin Informationen über einen Popstar entnehmen.	TB A2b WB A1	98 74			
	Ich kann einen Comic über ein Popkonzert verstehen.	TB A6 WB A4	100 76			
	Ich kann Anzeigen schnell überfliegen, um einen Eindruck zu bekommen, worum es geht.	TB B1b	102			
Sprechen monologisch	Ich kann einen Film- oder Popstar mit Hilfe eines Posters vorstellen.	TB A3	99			
	Ich kann berichten, was mein Partner in London unternehmen möchte.	WB B2	80			
	Ich kann eine Präsentation über einen Tag in London halten.	WB B3	80			
	Ich kann ein Bild beschreiben.	TB B4a WB B5	104 81			
Sprechen dialogisch	Ich kann mich über meine Lieblingsmusik unterhalten.	TB A1	98			
	Ich kann Vorschläge machen, was ich mit einem Besucher unternehmen könnte.	TB B3	104			
Schreiben	Ich kann über einen Popstar schreiben.	TB A2	98			
	Ich kann schriftlich meine Meinung begründen, wenn ich dazu Hilfen bekomme.	WB B2	80			
	Ich kann einen Text zu einem Gemälde schreiben, wenn ich Hilfen bekomme.	TB B5 WB B6	105 82			
	Ich kann einen Flyer über eine Veranstaltung schreiben.	TB P4	109			
Sprachmittlung	Ich kann Informationen aus einer Anzeige auf Deutsch wiedergeben.	WB B1	79			
Lern- und Arbeitstechniken	Ich kann eine Collage über meinen Lieblingsstar erstellen.	TB A3	99			
	Ich kann Lautschrift lesen, um zu erkennen, um welches Wort es sich handelt.	WB A9a	78			
Wortschatz	Ich kann Wörter zum Thema Musik in einem *word web* sammeln.	WB A8c	78			
Sprachliche Mittel	Ich kann auf Englisch wiedergeben, was jemand sagt und dabei die Pronomen anpassen.	TB A7 TB P3	101 108			
	Ich kann *may* und *might* verwenden, um Vermutungen zu äußern.	TB P5	109			

Was ich nach *Theme 8* schon kann

	Ich kann ...	**Material**		✔ Das kann ich gut.	O Das fällt mir noch schwer.	— Das kann ich noch nicht.
		Aufgabe	Seite			
Hören	Ich kann einem Gespräch über Urlaubspläne Informationen entnehmen.	TB A7 TB A9	117 118			
	Ich kann einem Lied entnehmen, wohin die Person reisen möchte.	TB A3	114			
	Ich kann einem Interview mit Reisenden entnehmen, woher sie kommen und was ihre Pläne sind.	TB B1b	119			
	Ich kann beim Hören Sätze markieren, die in dem Hörtext vorkommen.	WB A5	87			
Lesen	Ich kann einer Webseite Informationen entnehmen.	TB A6	116			
	Ich kann einen Dialog so gut verstehen, dass ich die vermischten Redebeiträge wieder in die richtige Reihenfolge bringen kann.	WB A6	87			
Sprechen monologisch	Ich kann über meine Pläne für die Ferien sprechen.	TB A1	114			
	Ich kann über eigene Erfahrungen mit dem Thema „Ferien ohne Eltern" berichten.	TB A10	118			
	Ich kann einen kurzen Vortrag halten, der mit dem Thema Urlaub zu tun hat.	WB A11	89			
Sprechen dialogisch	Ich kann mit Hilfe einer Rollenkarte ein Gespräch mit einem Reisenden führen.	WB A7	88			
	Ich kann ein Interview vorspielen, das ich gut vorbereitet habe.	TB B7c	123			
	Ich kann mit einem Partner ein Verkaufsgespräch vorspielen.	WB A6	87			
Schreiben	Ich kann einen Text über Familienbesuche in anderen Städten oder Ländern schreiben, wenn ich Hilfen bekomme.	TB A2	114			
	Ich kann Fragen für ein Interview aufschreiben.	TB B7	123			
	Ich kann darüber schreiben, welche Länder ich auf einer Weltreise besuchen und was ich dort tun würde.	WB B5 1.	92			
Lern- und Arbeitstechniken	Ich kann in der *wordbank* Wörter zum Thema *travelling* nachschlagen.	TB A2 WB A11	114 89			
	Ich kann die Bedeutung von Wörtern im Wörterbuch nachschlagen.	TB A10 TB P4	118 125			
Wortschatz	Ich kann Nomen passende Verben zuordnen.	WB A2	85			
	Ich kann Wörter in Gruppen sortieren.	TB P4	125			
	Ich kann eine Liste mit Redewendungen aufschreiben, die ich bei Reisen gebrauchen kann, auch wenn das Thema nicht so intensiv vorbereitet wurde.	TB A5 WB A5	115 87			
Sprachliche Mittel	Ich kann sagen, was jemand unter bestimmten Bedingungen tun würde, wenn ich Hilfen bekomme.	TB A4 WB A3	115 86			
	Ich kann sagen, wie lange jemand schon etwas macht, wenn ich Hilfen bekomme.	TB B2 WB B1	120 90			

Was mir in Klasse 7 beim Englischlernen geholfen hat:

HÖREN

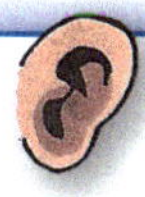

Hörtexte verstehe ich besonders gut, wenn ich

- ☐ vorweg eine Idee habe, worum es gehen könnte.
- ☐ den Text dazu mitlesen kann.
- ☐ mir beim Hören Notizen mache.
- ☐ dazu Bilder sehe.
- ☐ ______________________________

SPRECHEN

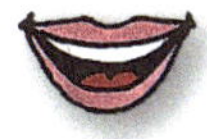

Sprechen kann ich besonders gut, wenn ich

- ☐ einen Dialog mit einem/r Partner/in führe.
- ☐ mir vorher Notizen mache.
- ☐ etwas auswendig lerne.
- ☐ viel über ein Thema gelesen habe.
- ☐ ______________________________

SCHREIBEN

Schreiben kann ich besonders gut, wenn ich

- ☐ mich an eine Vorlage oder einen *model text* halte.
- ☐ mir erstmal Notizen mache.
- ☐ meinen Text später durchsehen und bearbeiten kann.
- ☐ ______________________________

LESEN

Lesetexte verstehe ich besonders gut, wenn ich

- ☐ mir vor dem Lesen Bilder und Überschriften ansehe.
- ☐ mir vorher überlegt habe, was wahrscheinlich im Text vorkommen wird.
- ☐ den Text mit einem/r Partner/in besprechen kann.
- ☐ mir beim Lesen Notizen mache.
- ☐ ______________________________

WORTSCHATZ

Wörter lerne ich besonders gut, wenn ich

- ☐ sie in einem *word web* aufschreibe.
- ☐ sie oft laut vorspreche.
- ☐ etwas dazu aufzeichne.
- ☐ sie häufig wiederhole.
- ☐ ______________________________

GRAMMATIK

Grammatik verstehe ich besonders gut, wenn

- ☐ mir jemand die Regel erklärt.
- ☐ ich die Regel selbst herausfinde und sie aufschreibe.
- ☐ ich die Regel nachschaue, z. B. im LiF.
- ☐ ______________________________

Das habe ich in diesem Jahr besonders gern gemacht:

____

____

LiF 20 may, might

- **may** kann, ähnlich wie **can**, ausdrücken, dass etwas erlaubt ist:
  You may help the band with their gig at the weekend.
- **may** kann auch einen förmlichen Wunsch einleiten, so wie das deutsche möge:
  And may God's love be with you.
- **may** kann auch bedeuten, dass etwas möglich ist:
  That may be exciting.
- Wenn die Möglichkeit weniger realistisch erscheint, benutzt man **might**:
  That might be true.

- Man kann **might** auch verwenden, wenn man über etwas spekuliert:
  The man in the picture might be the grandfather.
- **may** und **might** stehen immer mit einem Hauptverb im Infinitiv.

LiF 21 Bedingungssätze 2 ● conditional clauses 2

- Bedingungssätze können realistische oder unrealistische Bedingungen nennen:

  You'll make Aunt Elsie very happy if you buy her that picture.

  Hier ist die Bedingung erfüllbar, denn Rosemary braucht das Bild nur für die Tante zu kaufen.

  If I had an aunt in London, I would visit her and go to the London Eye.

  Wer das sagt, hat *keine* Tante in London, sonst würde er oder sie anders reden. Die Bedingung für einen solchen Besuch in London ist also nicht erfüllbar, die Idee bleibt ein Wunschtraum.

- Mit einem Bedingungssatz kannst du also auch ausdrücken, was unter einer nur gedachten Bedingung passieren würde oder könnte. Dabei geht es um Ereignisse, die unwahrscheinlich oder unmöglich sind:

  If I had a lot of money, I would go to New York.

- Bei dieser zweiten Art von Bedingungssätzen steht der if-Satz im *simple past*. Im Hauptsatz steht *would, could* oder *might* – mit einem Hauptverb im Infinitiv.

IF-CLAUSE		MAIN CLAUSE	
If I had a friend in Australia,	**I**	**would** **could** **might**	**visit her.**

- Aufgepasst! Bei if-Sätzen heißt es manchmal *If I were …*, aber du kannst auch *If I was …* sagen. Beide Formen sind hier möglich.

  If I were rich, I would buy a fast car.

LiF 22 Die Verlaufsform im Perfekt ● present perfect progressive

- Wenn du sagen willst, wie lange etwas schon dauert, was immer noch nicht zu Ende ist, musst du die Verlaufsform im Perfekt benutzen:

How long have you been travelling?

I've been travelling from Melbourne for twenty-four hours.

- Dazu brauchst du **have been** oder **has been** und die ing-Form des Verbs.

LiF 23 Zeitangaben mit for

- Wenn du sagen willst, wie lange etwas gedauert hat, benutzt du eine Zeitangabe mit **for**:

I've been learning English for three years.

I've had my new bike for six months.